INSTANT SKIING
INSTANT FUN

Skiboards: Best Kept
Secret on the Slopes

Richard L. Roberts, PhD.

Instant Skiing, Instant Fun
Skiboards: Best Kept Secret on the Slopes

Published by Windrider Institute, LLC
Carson City, Nevada 89701

ISBN 978-0-9831316-0-1

Disclaimer/Legal Notices

While every attempt has been made to verify the information provided in this report, the author does not assume any responsibility for errors, inaccuracies or omissions. Any slights of people or organizations are unintentional. This book is not intended for use as a source of psychological or health related advice. You should be aware of any laws that govern skiing activity specific to your country, state and local ski resort.

Every effort has been made to accurately represent the product and its potential. The testimonials and examples used are from real people, but their experiences may not apply to the average person and are not intended to represent or guarantee that anyone will achieve the same or similar results. Each individual's success depends on his or her background, dedication, desire and motivation. As with any active endeavor, there is an inherent risk of loss of capital or potential injury. There is no guarantee that you will be successful in skiing or self-actualizing using any of the ideas or products sold by Richard L. Roberts, Ph.D., Skiboards Superstore, Inc., its related websites and the publisher, Windrider Institute Press.

Library of Congress Control Number: 2011941993
Library of Congress subject headings:

Skiing
Skis
Sports Psychology

Table of Contents

PART II: Instant Skiing

Part III: Grooving With Gravity

Part IV: Skiboarding and Self-Actualization

In the Zone: Self-Actualization and the Destabilization of Paradigm Paralysis. An Exploratory Study of the Embodied Total Attention Experience, By Doc Roberts

Acknowledgements

First, I'd like to thank all of our customers since our beginning days in 1997, who ride skiboards throughout the world. It's been such a delight to get to know you and in some small way, contribute to your enhanced enjoyment of life. You've inspired me and taught me much about the willingness to try new things, while not caring what others think. Thank you for sharing your ideas, experiences, testimonials, photos and support.

I would like to thank the following people. Thank you Herschel, wherever you are skating and riding, for getting me on skiboards that first time and for all the fun times we had discovering new ways to ride them. As well I would like to thank my skating crew who joined me in this new adventure back in the late 90's. Sasha, you've been a constant source of inspiration and best friend. You've kept me going all these years with your experience and enthusiasm for the sport and your friendship. My thanks also goes out to TC, Carol and Taylor and the many others who worked with me to build this business and enlighten the world.

Thanks goes to my many programmers and business advisors, making the website what it is today. A very special thanks to Whitney, who so graciously donated her time to edit my book and polish it, so it could more accurately reveal what I really wanted to communicate. I wouldn't consider myself a writer, just someone passionate about skiboards, and as such, her assistance in organizing my thoughts and putting them into a more user-friendly format is greatly appreciated.

Lastly, I would like to thank Divine intervention for guiding me along this path and providing the necessary solutions to the many business type challenges that came my way. Unfolding of one's potential sure comes in mysterious ways sometimes. I'm happy to serve the many who now ride skiboards, and those who are about to discover the simplicity and joy of this awesome sport.

Richard (Doc) Roberts, PhD.

Preface

It seems that when something new comes over the horizon, at first, most people are hesitant to try it. They want others to be the guinea pigs I guess. Yet, there are always those relative few who will step out of the box and embrace it with a sense of adventure and excitement. These 'out-of-the-boxers' recognize something, though sometimes perhaps they can't even understand the attraction logically. They just have to try it, no matter what others think.

My actual first experience with skiboards occurred in the spring of 1997. Skating through the streets of downtown Denver with my friend Herschel one evening, he began to tell me about these 'new short skis.' He said they were called *Big Foots* and that he heard they felt like skating on the slopes. We had skied together many times, and of course spent years skating together, so I totally trusted his intuition.

It just so happened that another skating friend had a couple of pairs of Big Foots. So we borrowed them, and Herschel and I headed to Eldora Ski Resort, outside of Boulder, Colorado. It had just snowed about 8 inches that night so there was plenty of fresh powder to play in. I strapped them on my ski boots that morning and up the lift we went (neither one of us having any idea what to expect).

Getting off the lift, I must say at first, I was a bit anxious. After all, it seemed like this was something so very different from anything else I had done before. We headed down the slopes. He was a little ahead of me and shouted back, "Think skating, not skiing." So I did, and I could not believe the thrill that ran through my body. From my very first run, it felt so familiar. It was more like dancing or skating than skiing. It truly was outrageous fun right from the first run.

I also really liked that I could stand upright and ride the slopes without poles and with a naturalness that was definitely missing in my experience with skis. Yet, there was something indescribable about this experience also. With my background in vocational consulting, I immediately recognized the signs. It was destiny calling.

Imagine, playing on snow, being in the mountains, with absolute abandon because you're totally in control, able to stop and turn as easily as you might if you were walking. It took only one run to know without a doubt that I had found a new sport that I would be doing a lot more of. It was that quick – just one run! My friend concurred. I became an evangelist for this new sport after my very first day!

As I couldn't contain my enthusiasm, I told practically everyone I ran into. Skiboarding was contagious and almost everyone I told immediately wanted to try these too. I soon began arranging access to demo 'skiboards' (this term was not identified until 1998) and even taking groups up to the mountain in Breckenridge, Colorado and WinterPark, Colorado. Their experience was consistently the same – absolute total fun from the first day! They were as hooked as I was, within a matter of a few runs.

Right from my first day, skiboarding ignited a new sense of passion and freedom. What was surprising though was that it seemed to carryover into my everyday life as well. Best way I can describe it was that it was an awakening. This awakening was accompanied by feelings of liberation and vitality. While I had this experience in many out-of-the-box adventures throughout my life, this feeling of total freedom in skiing was something quite new.

To me the real essence of this unique sport is breaking through old, outdated mindsets, and snapping me out of my almost trance-like daily routine. I began to experience a sense expansion beyond previous invisible limitations. What I know from my background in consulting is that this is the domain of peak experiences and living to our full potential (that which we all secretly yearn for). While skiboards represent a new tool for riding the ski slopes, I know that they also offer the opportunity for this accelerated personal transformation, which I'll explore with you in the following pages.

Back to my story. I began researching online to find other brands of skiboards besides the Big Foots. I found only a couple of companies online that were making parabolic wood core twin tips. I contacted them, got a few pairs to lend out to friends (and maybe sell a few pairs) and started a small website. I was so enthusiastic I had to tell the world about these. I had already exhausted my wife and friends with my constant excitement about them, so I needed to find a bigger audience anyway.

My intention was to launch a website just as a little side business to inform the world and perhaps to entice other companies to start making them. The internet was just getting started then. Since there was no official name for them yet, I created my website under the name of Powder Skates, because that is what they felt like to me.

So with a small stock of powder skates and my six page website live, I began spreading the word about this new sport. I also began selling a few pairs on a weekly basis to my surprise and even had to start reordering more as a result. My inventory kept growing and the phones kept ringing.

A year later, I found myself with an ever expanding website, more product in inventory, and daily UPS pickups. My dream to share my enthusiasm of skiboarding with others turned into a full time business. When the name 'skiboards' was officially decided sometime around 1998, I created Skiboards.com.

Here I was busy pursuing my career as a Human Potential Consultant after just receiving my Ph.D. I had plans to finish my book, be on the travel circuit offering my seminars and maybe even be famous someday. However, life apparently had other ideas, as it often does.

In just a few short years, my garage was converted into a warehouse and five phone lines were installed in my home. I was barely able to keep up with orders. I was buying, selling, managing the website, packing, shipping and handling customer support. As it rapidly got overwhelming, I began hiring others to help me. The business has been busy ever since, all thanks to the simple joy of riding skiboards.

Started in 1997, The Skiboards Superstore, Inc. (dba Skiboards .com) has now grown into the world's largest skiboard retail business. The Superstore has offered skiboards from manufacturers including Salomon, K2, Atomic, Line, Canon, Groove, Line, Klimax, Kneissl, Microski, Fischer, Alpina, Groove, Head, Kissmark, Karhu, Journey, Blizzard, Elan, Summit and many more.

Skiboards.com also now manufactures its own brand of skiboards under the Summit Skiboards name. Summit Skiboards is focused on the design and manufacture of high performance, top-of-the-line skiboards. Skiboards.com also sells its own brand of skiboarding accessories, including gear bags, tune kits, carry bags, base waxes and more.

What sometimes surprises me is that I still feel the same passion now as I did when I first rode them. The passion is really con-tagious. The more people I tell about it, the more I receive testimonials from customers who are having the same experience as I am. Enthusiasm, passion, freedom, fun, and joy – these are the common experiences of skiboarders all over the world.

Interestingly, my experience with skiboarding directly exhibits the same characteristics that I had discovered in my research in human potential psychology of those living to their greater human potential. My career previously was involved with teaching others, including corporate workforces, how to realize their full creative potential, so it was very familiar to me. These peak experiences have deeper psychological and transfor-mational implications and I'll be exploring these with you in the following pages.

In my many years of experience with skiboards, I've come to develop a great appreciation, not only for the fun of riding them, but more so, for the personal breakthroughs that occur regularly during and after the experience. Skiboards represent a liberation from old habits, fears and limitations in riding on the slopes. As compared to long skis, skiboards allow greater creative freedom and naturally allow our own unique individuality to fully emerge without restraint.

In my personal experience, and that of an ever growing community of worldwide skiboarders, riding skiboards adds a whole new dimension to the sport of snow riding. For those who love immediate gratification, this is the ticket. Only go on vacation once a year or two, and don't want to spend your time in lessons? Skiboards are the solution. Best of all, skiboards create the experience of exhilaration, joy and those peak moments that until now were only experienced by the crème of the crop skiers and snowboarders.

To learn to ski instantly, or improve your skills fast, whether already a skier or a beginner, skiboards have something to teach you. However, there's so much more that skiboards offer. The breakthroughs that are experienced on the mountain also carry over into everyday life. This is the greatest advantage and truly the best kept secret of all.

If you're looking for a new challenge, a true adventure or just want to feel the gusto of living on the edge of your creative potential, I strongly encourage you to give skiboards a try (if you haven't already). Welcome to a whole new life adventure.

Richard L. Roberts, Ph.D.
President
Skiboards Superstore, Inc.
http://skiboards.com

PART I

First, Let's Talk Skiboards

It's sheer joy. You usually have a big smile on your face all day. It all just flows so easily. I would say the term peak experience is pretty accurate to describe skiboarding.
- Mary's first time -

I had to tell someone! I'm not a writer of testimonials, but the experience is an awesome high. What a sport!
- Dave -

In some ways, skiboarding is a more pure and therefore more satisfying experience.
- Posted on the Skiboards.com Forum -

CHAPTER 1

What are Skiboards?

Imagine the freedom that comes with going anywhere you want, backwards, forwards, in the trees, diving off the lift chair (just kidding). Skiers - no more worries about crossing tips or catching them on those pesky moguls. Forget all those beginner, intermediate and advanced level signs. My wife at the time, a confirmed blue run (intermediate) skier, who would have never progressed much further without big bucks invested in lessons, was skiboarding double black glades after two runs!
- Doc Roberts -

Let's face it, not everyone finds skiing to be fun, especially when starting out. Consider the lessons, awkward moments on the hill, the occasional crossing of the tips, and of course, lugging all that equipment. Skis, like snowboards, have a relatively long learning curve. It seems even longer when we would just rather be having fun cruising the slopes and enjoying our day instead.

Well, good news, the thrill is back. Wait until you try skiboards! These new snow riding tools and the suggestions I have to offer will not only improve your long ski skills, if that is your preference, but also blow you away with how much fun they are and how much freedom skiboards provide. No matter whether you're a beginner, advanced or expert rider, skiboards will open up totally new possibilities for excitement on the mountain.

Unlike long skis, the speed of skill acquisition with skiboards is remarkably fast. Whatever ability level we're at, everyone gets to enjoy a literal breakthrough experience on the slopes. These are truly a total blast from the very first day, with remarkably less fear while offering much greater control.

Skiboards carve like snowboards, ride with the freedom of inline skates, totally jam through moguls and turn the black diamond glade runs into a playground, not to mention all the tricks and jumps you can pull off in the terrain parks. Skiboarding is the perfect crossover sport for skaters of all types, while offering a whole new fun adventure for skiers and snowboarders.

Skiboards are extremely easy to learn. All that's needed is ski boots and a desire to experience an exciting new adventure. Chuck the poles! Don't need lessons. Skiers, skaters, snowboarders – listen up – you already possess the necessary skills to do this. You'll be amazed at how fast you're up and jamming on these.

Combining the same advanced technologies of skis and snowboards, skiboards (a. k. a. snowblades, Ski Boards, ski blades, skiblades, short skis and miniskis) are about half the length of skis, ranging from about 65 cm to 125 cm in length (though skiboards.com also offers models up to 143cm in length). Skiboards come in a variety of shapes and widths, from narrow to wide, mostly featuring wood cores and twin tips. These come in pairs, just like with long skis.

Skiboards can be mounted with either non-release or release ski-type bindings. These bindings fit regular ski boots. Depending on the bindings, skiboards can also be used with mountaineering, AT and hard-shell snowboard boots. As skiboards allow anyone to have a more upright stance, high performance boots are not necessary. Just find boots that are more upright and definitely comfortable.

Skiboards can also be mounted with snowboard bindings and used with snowboard boots. This requires a 4 hole standard insert pattern, that some skiboards come with. Now snowboarders can easily try out skiboards, buying them without bindings and then attaching their own bindings. However, we also offer snowboard bindings on our website.

Riding skiboards is a very different feeling than riding longer skis or snowboards. The name skiboards reflects the way they capture the positive aspects of both. While there are two of them, like skis, and parallel turns are made like on long skis, the higher performance models are made with the twin-tip construction of snowboards. This allows for greater speed, including those thrilling lay-it-over-carves. Being shorter, ski-boards give the feeling of skating, more than skiing. It's almost like having two small snowboards on our feet.

However, unlike skis and snowboards, the learning curve is dramatically faster. My experience is that most people learn in one day at most, without lessons. For those who've skied or ever skated (ice, inline or quad), it will only take a few runs to get it. While it's still recommended that first timers take a lesson or two just to get used to getting on and off the lift, most total beginners can get it from a few suggestions I offer in this book. Those who already ski can just go right up to more advanced runs and will know how to do it right away. Just don't lean forward.

Skiboards handle the same conditions and terrain as the long sticks, including powder, glades, moguls, terrain parks, backcountry and more. Skiboards ride quite differently than skis, with a much shorter turning radius, faster stopping power and more control. Being the shortest and lightest of all snow riding tools, skiboards are easy to carry to the lift, easy to ship and easy to travel with.

What Skiing Magazine had to say about skiboards as compared to conventional planks, is: "Skiboards, sometimes called 'snow-blades' after Salomon's models, are incredibly easy to use and great for learning to ski. They're especially insane when it comes to new-school tricks." Had skiboards been invented first, who knows if the slopes would be so populated by long skis?

While alpine skis feature release bindings, other snow riding equipment such as snowboards, cross country and telemark skis use non-release bindings. Skiboards can be mounted with either non-release bindings or conventional step-in release ski bindings (as well as snowboard bindings). Studies have shown that skiboards are the safest snow riding tools on the mountain, especially when mounted with traditional, brand name, unmodified release ski bindings and correctly adjusted.

Of course, if you're a ski racer, then there's nothing faster than a good set of race-specific racing skis. However, the vast majority of us (especially those who only get so many vacations a year) do not need downhill race skis, or the latest and best ski equipment for that matter. Skiboards may not be as fast as long skis if heading straight down the mountain without turning, however they're much faster than might be expected particularly when riding the wider platform skiboards. The wide skiboards have more surface area and as a result, have more glide and floatation. Skiboarders often remark that they're passing most skiers on the slopes, due to the shorter turning radius (as compared to longer radius turns on skis) and extra surface area.

For the majority of recreational skiers, skiboards offer incredible advantages. They require less effort than long skis, are easier to maneuver and even allow for more graceful cruising on the run. It's the design and construction of skiboards that make the entire mountain accessible, right from day one. Any size or type will do really, though different sizes and shapes make forever expanding opportunities for fun.

I've found that once people try skiboards, their whole perspective on riding 'shorties' shifts. Be prepared, because like the majority of customers, those long skis may soon become dust collectors or get made into furniture. Yet, giving up the skis is not necessary, as skiboards can be a great alternative fun tool to ride besides skis and/or snowboards.

Think how good it would be for ski resorts. Skiboards make it fun and easy to ride the slopes, and as a result, customers would most certainly come back more often. Having had so much fun, they tell their friends and family about it and bring even more people to the mountain. Skiboards, being a true long ski alternative, definitely increase the enthusiasm for returning to the slopes. Most new skiboarders report that they never even bought season passes before, until they began skiboarding.

Wow, do skiboards bring an immediate smile to your face. Designed for all age riders, from beginning to expert, skiboards just take one day to awaken to new possibilities for fun. Since having fun on the slopes is generally the priority of most snow riders, skiboards really deliver the goods and fast. That is why I often use the phrase – *Pure Fun from Day One!*

Skiboards are not to be confused with the *graduated learning method* used in the 50's to train would-be skiers on shorter planks (chopped off skis). The GLM method was introduced with the intention of gradually introducing beginners to longer and longer skis. This method was adopted by many for a time to introduce newcomers to skis.

Clif Taylor was the man most often credited with this method. However, he did not really advocate this approach of graduating to longer skis. He believed in, and only rode, short skis, with his preferred models being 76 cm and 120 cm in length. With these two lengths, he believed you had all you needed to ride in any conditions and terrain.

I would not equate these short skis with the beginning of skiboarding. Clif only made chopped off skis that were straight and narrow, with no side cut. Bindings were not very sophisticated either. This was not the beginning of the sport of skiboarding. His short skis, though quite popular, never evolved into higher performance designs that could handle all mountain terrain and conditions. These were truly lacking, as compared to the advanced technology of today's skiboards.

However, for those who want to improve their long ski skills, skiboards do present the perfect opportunity for advancing even quicker, similar to the graduated learning method. This means, start on skiboards, and then graduate to long skis and anyone can experience immediate improvement. Skiboards promote proper centering and balance. As a result, progress is faster than just continuing to tough it out on long skis. I have heard from numerous ski race teams that use skiboards to train on, for this very reason.

A Brief History of Skiboards

The origin of the sport of riding these shorties can be traced to the introduction of two products – first, Kneissl's Big Foot and second, the Atomic Figl. Both were designed to make riding on snow easier. In the case of the Big Foot, complete with toes and a designated right and left foot, these were mounted with non-release composite bindings from the factory that fit regular ski boots. Big Foots were 65 cm in length and constructed with a foam core. These were first introduced in the mid-1970's and sold every year up to 2007, when they were discontinued. Estimates are that over a million pairs were sold throughout the world.

In 1982, Atomic introduced the Figl at 63.5 cm. The Atomic Figl featured factory mounted, composite bindings and were made with a foam core as well, along with sintered bases and Rockwell steel edges. These were designed specifically for European mountain climbers to ride the glaciers back down after climbing. They were also used by those who wanted to ice skate on the frozen lakes. Soon after, the name changed to the Atomic Maxi Carve.

There were not many other similar products introduced until the late 1990s, allowing the Big Foot and Figl to dominate this specialized market. Perhaps partly around the enthusiasm for these 'short skis', 'shorties' began to appear around 1997. These new designs began to incorporate more versatile features like wood cores, symmetrical twin tips and parabolic shapes. Companies like Canon, Line, Groove, Microski and Klimax began producing their own styles of these unique short boards.

Kent Keiswieller, the designer of Microski, created his Microskis by modifying snowboard designs. Eventually, Keiswieller designed the MicroSki at 68 cm with factory mounted non-release bindings. These rode similar to Big Foots, but without the toes, and with more side cut and an improved flex (Big Foots do not flex). They were quite popular, even in the ski schools.

The appeal of these new short skis was that they were simpler to learn how to ride on snow. Many customers remarked on how similar they were to skating. On these, people could make quick turns, fast stops and still remain in control at speed. As a result, many skaters of all types began to get interested in riding them. In these, beginners found a tool to learn to ski quickly, thus allowing them to explore the entire mountain with less fear and more confidence, while sporting a huge smile on their face.

In February, 1998, the term 'skiboards' became official. This name was chosen based on the construction and riding style of short skis in a meeting of the existing skiboard manufacturers. Skiboards were made to carve on edge like snowboards with parabolic twin tip shapes, yet since they came in pairs – one for each foot – that were also like skis. Some people still spell them "Ski Boards" as a result, though like the words 'Snowboards' and 'Snowshoes' for example, "skiboards" without the space is the correct spelling.

A flood of new products emerged in the 1998-99 season. During this time, Journey Skiboards, a local Colorado company, introduced their hand made, 87 cm wood core twin tips with a hemp top sheet and sintered bases. These made quite a splash with their custom design top sheets. Skiboards.com had exclusive designs created that included the Deep Forest, Red Racer, Psychedelic and Woodie, to name a few. Line, Microski, Klimax, Canon and Groove continued to expand their models during this season. Larger ski companies, such as Salomon, Atomic and Blizzard introduced their own unique models as well. As with any emerging sport, there was much experimentation in the early days, featuring differing side cuts, construction, shapes and bindings. Salomon even came out with a few wood core, wide-body models including metal bindings.

Many manufacturers began incorporating stainless steel inserts in their skiboards to accommodate interchangeable higher performance, more durable, non-release bindings with better power transfer. For example, Line introduced their CAM and Pro model aluminum bindings that mounted to these four hole insert patterns (40 mm X 40 mm). Bomber Industries, another

Colorado company, introduced their high end all aluminum and stainless steel, skiboard-specific, non-release binding called the Toaster. Canon introduced their own 4 hole binding.

For the 1999-2000 season, Elan jumped on board with their all new Roller Ski, a short twin tip skiboard that came with factory mounted non-release bindings. Fischer Skis introduced their Spyder 98 cm asymmetrical skiboards with factory mounted non-release bindings. Dynastar also entered the market with 85 cm and 99 cm wider, twin tip wood core boards that were quite popular. Snowjam introduced two models, the 75 cm and 85 cm short skis with non-release bindings. Salomon also began producing a few more models of skiboards that were wider as well as narrower models in 90 cm and 99 cm lengths. While still classifying them as skiboards, Salomon named their particular version of skiboards, *Snowblades*.

For the 2000 and 2001 season, Alpina, Atomic, Microski, Canon, Fischer, Elan, Dynastar, Salomon, Line, Groove, K2, Journey, Odyssey, Snowjam, Kneissl, and Kissmark had all introduced new skiboard models. All of these companies offered either factory mounted non-release bindings or provided four stainless steel inserts to mount other available non-release bindings. One of the great products I felt, though short lived, was Atomic's wood core, wide-body twin tips in 85 cm length. This was an innovation for them and a smooth riding pair of skiboards. These were only produced for one season and unfortunately in small quantities. They were red, black and white mounted with Atomic non-release bindings.

During this time, Bomber Industries introduced their new Elite non-release bindings, made of aluminum and stainless steel that mounted to all skiboards with the 40 mm by 40 mm mounting pattern. These also had bumpers under the toe and heel that provided greater carving ability and enhanced dampening. With the improved flex of the skiboards and total power transfer from boot to board, Bombers proved very popular and still are to this day.

The market, though still small, was building up steam with greater national publicity, competition events in the X-Games and full length videos from Frontside Films featuring many big air tricks, grinding and footage of riders pushing the envelope of the sport. Canon Industries introduced their Black Tape video which demonstrated the many ways people were riding skiboards – including through the trees, in the half pipes, deep powder, doing lay over carving and of course, big air tricks. The Black Tape is still viewable on the Skiboards.com website and our Youtube page. One of the biggest contributors to this growing national recognition was Salomon, however, who got their snowblades into many ski resort rental shops throughout the country. This made it much simpler for people to try them.

Head/Tyrolia joined the market in the 2001 and 2002 season. Head introduced their 94 cm Headliner, a wood core, asymmetrical twin tip, with factory mounted Tyrolia Sympro 4 bindings. These were the first step-in, release bindings used on skiboards. This particular model was a huge hit, even though at first was only intended for junior skiboarders and not adults with larger boot sizes. This has since changed (perhaps due to my suggestions) and now they're made for adult riders with adult bindings. The 94cm Head's became more popular than ever as a result and continue to be available each season.

Over time, many of the smaller, as well as some of the larger manufacturers, dropped out of the market. Companies such as Salomon, Line, Groove, Canon, Alpina, Dynastar, Journey, Microski and a few others stopped producing skiboards. The reasons for this are diverse, but often it was due to their cheaper construction (trying to make a buck at the expense of performance). For example, Salomon's later snowblade models were made with foam cores and a narrow width construction. These were great for groomed runs, but not great for speed or powder. As a result, skiboards got a bad reputation as being wobbly, and being good only for beginners.

Some companies dropped out due to financial issues and mismanagement. Others succumbed to the long ski mindset (like Line), discussed later, and decided to only manufacture traditional skis. Journey, who was making handmade, one-at-a-time skiboards, simply could not keep up with demand and folded.

The sport has come a long way from these early years, though. Some of the bigger ski companies, such as Head, Elan, Atomic, K2, Snowjam and others are still producing skiboards and continue to stretch the boundaries of the sport. While the variety of choices aren't like they used to be, the quality and performance of skiboards has dramatically improved with much more refinement thanks to these prior years of experimentation.

A major trend in the sport that evolved a few years back is mounting skiboards with release bindings. This dramatically increases the safety factor for skiboards without inhibiting performance. It also opens the market to skiers who are more familiar with ski bindings. While in the earlier years of skiboarding, these ski bindings did have a tendency to inhibit flex and were quite heavy, they have since evolved to allow greater flex with lighter weights. People also liked that these bindings were easier to adjust than non-release bindings and of course, the ease of step in and step out (a huge advantage over non-release bindings) is quite a hit.

While skiboards can still be mounted with non-release bindings, the trend is moving towards release bindings because they perform just as well or even better. The bindings produced by the major ski companies, such as Atomic, Salomon, Tyrolia, Rossignol and Elan are tested, reliable and certified to perform. They will not release prematurely, if the release factor (DIN) is adjusted properly, but, more important, they release when essential.

Seeing the need for pushing the envelope of this sport even farther, I made the decision in 2004 to start designing and manufacturing my own, higher performance skiboards. Summit Skiboards, Inc. began producing various models starting with the 85 cm twin tip to further expand the terrain and conditions that skiboards could perform on. This 85 cm model was soon followed by a 99 cm and 110 cm.

My desire for this company was and is to create the highest performing skiboards on the market, and further, to have them truly rival snowboards and skis as snow riding tools. To date, Summit models include the Jade 87 cm, Headwall 95 cm, Freedom 99 cm, Nomad 99 cm, Custom 110 cm, and the Marauder 125 cm. All these can be mounted with release bindings, while the Jade 87, Nomad 99 and Custom 110 also include inserts for mounting of non-release and snowboard bindings as well.

The sport of skiboarding never really made it mainstream. Even though there was significant publicity in the early days, no longer does the ski industry really mention skiboards, nor will we likely find them in most retail sports stores or ski resort rental shops. As many larger companies have dropped out of this sport, publicity has waned.

What I see though is that this sport has essentially achieved true cult status in that it spreads by word of mouth. There is a passionate 'in crowd.' I personally like that skiboarding operates under the radar. The purity of the sport has remained in tact as a result. Skiboards won't be showing up in Walmart or other mass quantity retail chains anytime soon. This is especially good because they would be most likely made with cheaper construction and people would not get to experience the full potential of this great sport.

Fortunately, there are still core companies committed to producing high quality, high performance skiboards, who see the possibilities of this sport for bringing people to the mountain. There is freedom inherent in riding skiboards with no prescribed methodologies. It's truly liberating to operate outside the confines of the conventional.

To me, the history of this sport is still being written and we're all a part of it. While many things have changed over the years, there continues to be an ever growing interest by adventurous souls around the world who're open to trying new ways to ride the slopes, preferring not to be limited by traditional equipment.

Though some may say that the sport is done, I find it comes mostly from those who have not really ridden high performance skiboards. The mass produced, cheaper construction skiboards made by the larger manufacturers in the early days served to turn off many people. The manufacturers mistakenly assumed that this meant the sport was dead.

I find in contrast that our customer base at Skiboards.com continues to grow year after year as more people find their way to skiboards. The unique advantages of skiboards continue to have a real appeal.

Instant Skiing and Instant Fun

It's my personal experience, as well as that of many, many skiboarders throughout the world that skiboarding represents a breakthrough in riding the slopes. This is a breakthrough like snowboards were a breakthrough when they first came out. It's not just skiing on short skis, but it's really more like skating on the slopes, allowing for a whole new skill set and individual creative expression.

This breakthrough is really due to the extremely short learning curve. Learning to master the equipment so quickly then sets the stage for total creative freedom on the slopes. The real transformation begins on the slopes when we're able to step out of the existing mindset of how we're supposed to be riding, or acting, for that matter. From there, these incredible feelings of liberation begin to carry over into the rest of our lives as well.

It's this recognition, even if perhaps only on the subconscious level, that creates the desire for more. After the first time riding skiboards, there is enough of a glimpse to see what's possible and crave more. Of course, anyone can have this experience in many, many ways, with many different recreational activities, but since this book is about my favorite sport, I'll be pointing out the advantages specific to riding skiboards.

Ultimately, what causes people to embrace this sport is the occurrence of powerful peak moments. Having a true peak experience is unmistakable and even life changing. Nothing compares to the feelings of flowing, oneness and joy, while physically engaged in effortless movement. Skiboards ignite this experience quite naturally, even from the first day, and usually every day after that. This is the instant fun part.

With the ability to ski instantly, there simply are more peak experiences happening from the beginning days than any other snow riding sport. This is true for beginners, as well as seasoned skiers. Even more, those who have these regular joyful moments find that something else occurs. They begin to disengage from limiting thought patterns and behaviors that have kept them operating at only a small fraction of their potential.

As one continues to ride skiboards, the process of breaking down these outworn physiological and psychological habit patterns continues quite naturally. Therefore, besides just downloading my knowledge and experience regarding skiboards, and my suggestions for accelerating the learning curve, I'll also be sharing deeper insights into the process of personal transformation associated with skiboarding.

CHAPTER 2

The Skiboard Advantage

I've got my own life to live. I'm the one that's gonna die when it's time for me to die, so let me live my life the way I want to.
- Jimi Hendrix –

Life must be lived as play.
- Plato -

Over the years, I've talked with great people from all over the world, and have heard all types of stories about their positive experiences riding skiboards. It truly is enjoyable for me to hear from customers. While there are numerous reasons why a person may choose to ride skiboards, I've found some primary motivators that are common to almost all. Here they are:

Skiboards are Much Easier to Ride than Skis or Snowboards!

Skiboards transcend the usual learning curve because they're easier to control, stop, turn and ride more than other snow riding equipment. Skiboards, being shorter, mean less chance of crossing or catching tips like with skis. Dancers, skaters, skiers, snowboarders, water skiers, and even walkers, anyone can usually learn in just a few runs without lessons. However, for those who've never been on a ski lift, it may take more like a day to get used to the mechanics of it all.

Experienced skiers, even snowboarders, are trying them. Skiboards stimulate the creative imagination, challenging us to invent new ways to glide and enjoy the mountain. As with any new sport, we also find a renewed connection to our bodies as we start to move in new ways. At the very least, this is a great break from the usual snow riding experience, a chance to experience something new and have an entirely new adventure.

Skiboarding literally allows anyone to go from beginner to fearless expert in a matter of days, not years. Yet, we get to experience the same freedom and exhilaration that longtime snow riders gain after many years of practice.

For first timers, the answer is easy: instant gratification! Skiboards offer beginners the shortest learning curve on the slopes. Skiboards make it easy to control speed and begin carving like a pro. With less length to manage and no tips to really cross, skiboards eliminate the awkwardness that beginners experience with long traditional skis. Turning and stopping are no longer a mystery, steep slopes aren't intimidating, powder is now a pleasure and moguls can be truly fun.

Some people say that using skiboards is cheating. They say it's necessary to pay our dues before we get to the good stuff! This is just the product of cultural conditioning that I'll be discussing later. No, we don't have to work hard to earn our turns. Why not have great times today?

Those who prefer to be more adventurous, even more rebellious, may be curious about another fun way to get down the mountain. Sure, it's new, even perhaps odd looking, compared to those long sticks. This I believe is only because skis came along first. Were it the other way around, skiboards would not look so strange and long skis would seem odd instead.

Intermediate skiers: Elevate your game to a new level. Sure, staying on the intermediate runs, maybe for the rest of your life, is still good wholesome fun. However, with skiboards, it's not necessary to be stuck there any longer. Now anyone can quickly venture into new, previously off limits terrain, with greater confidence and much less fear. Leave the 'intermediate rut' and easily explore more advanced terrain with greater confidence. What's remarkable is that this jumping up a new level can occur within just one day on skiboards. Imagine jumping up a level in just one day!

Steep mogul fields are no longer off limits. Pick a line and go. Tree skiing isn't the terror it once was. Jumping and performing tricks, usually reserved for experts, is now within the grasp of confirmed intermediate recreational skiers. Even powder becomes a joy.

Expert skiers: Here's the opportunity to master a new sport and take this sport to a new level. Carving a huge, laid over, high speed carve on a pair of skiboards, while dragging a hand in the snow is a whole new experience. Discover the rush of tree skiing at speeds rarely attempted on long skis. No limits, just pure freedom! In addition, skiboards will dramatically improve long ski skills, focusing the attention on more refined, centered balance and edging.

Skaters, this is your ultimate cross over sport. Anyone who has skated, even if they're not doing it now, find that when they get on skiboards, they almost instantly know how to do it. A large percentage of skiboard customers are skaters (roller, inline, hockey and ice) because skiboards are like skating on snow and the skills transfer easily. Skaters take to skiboards very quickly as compared to long skis, as the stance, balance and maneuvering provide a similar skate-like feel. This even includes those who used to skate, but haven't recently. No matter, the skills are still in body memory.

As mentioned earlier, this was my personal experience. As a long time skater I took to it immediately, as did all my skating buddies. I could not believe how similar it was to skating. Just go to a local rink, even if not a skater now, and skate a little. Skating will give an immediate feel of balance and turning, so hitting the slopes on skiboards will already feel familiar.

I got my kids to the local rink before they hit the slopes and my experience was the same with them. Once on skiboards, they took off like they already had done it many times before. I highly recommend skating as a way to get in shape for hitting the slopes as well.

Regarding the ease of riding skiboards, let's hear from the experience of some of our customers.

Dave from England offers this:

One of the commonest questions asked about skiboards is 'Are they a real alternative to skis?' This is a story about three ski bums who set out to find the answer. The cast: two expert male skiers, one female intermediate. The stage: the Italian Dolomites. The weapons: four different pairs of 99 cm carving skiboards. The plan, 6 days testing on the mountain in all conditions from groomed blues to off piste blacks. This was not to be about throwing tricks in the park. Most skiers don't do that! This was about miles, endless miles of gliding and carving, and maybe a little apres-ski.

The first thing we noticed was the very high quality of the boards. These are not cheap toys. They are beautifully made snow-riding tools. The bases and edges, graphics and finish, were all in line with top end skis. Considering the price, this came as a surprise. Second, they were so LIGHT! If you have ever spent a day lugging a pair of skis and poles around the rail stations of Europe, you will know what I mean! But what were they like on snow? In a word – fantastic! All of us were able to ride the boards from the first moment we tried, but it took about a day to fully settle in. At first they seemed unstable and twitchy, but we were skiers, what did we know?

Skiboards are NOT SKIS! The techniques for getting the best out of them are different. By the end of the first day we were all learning to weight both boards instead of only the downhill one, and stability had returned. We probably would have found it easier if we had never skied before! But the speeds these things can attain really caught us. We were all expecting a big slow down over our skis. Forget it. You only notice a difference on the almost flat sections where skis glide faster. This did not prove a problem however, as it is so easy to skate up to speed on skiboards. In those little areas where the piste slopes upward for a few yards, causing skiers to use their poles or sidestep, the skating ability of skiboards make skis look silly.
Day 2 was spent pushing harder and harder looking for the limits. Result: NO LIMITS! When the going gets really tough, steep mogul blacks, everyone agreed skiboards were safer than

skis. They don't catch, and they don't run away with you. Net result, you get down quicker and safer. On day 3, the plan was to ski a route called the Sella Ronda. This is a circular route that goes on for miles and miles, through villages and over cols. It takes a good skier about half a day, more if you get lost, or the lift queues are bad. The two expert skiers went, one on skis, and the other on skiboards. As for speed, there was absolutely no difference. The two were able to ski together all day, neither one having any particular advantage, until about three quarters of the way round, when the guy on the skis was starting to get tired. Oh dear, mark that one up to skiboards then! They really do require only a fraction of the effort.

By now it was becoming obvious that skiboards are indeed a very real alternative to skis, and as the week progressed we were able to discover more about the subtleties of this new sport. Things like 'popping' the tails out of turns to catapult you into the next, huge carved turns with one hand dragging in the snow, and linked turns so tight that the upper body continues straight down the fall line while the legs only swing from side to side like a pendulum. They are true whole mountain free ride tools, able to take you anywhere you want. Will we go back to our skis? The intermediate lady had dumped her full-length skis. Never wants to see them again. One of the male experts has done the same, the other wants to keep both. And about the apres-ski, what do you think?

Laura from Orange, Connecticut shares her experience:

I decided to try skiboarding after visiting the Skiboards.com website last year and reading the reviews and experiences of people who had tried it. I learned to ski at 35 and while I am an aggressive skier and improved enough to ski black diamonds, I never felt that I was a pretty skier. The poles always felt awkward and the times when I felt I had it all going on at the same time were few and far between. So I tried skiboards.

The first time down the slopes at Mount Snow I was clattering along, my feet bouncing up and down and I hated it. By the time I got to the end of the slope, I was starting to smile a little.

By the second run, the clattering and knee shaking was less, and by my third run, I was hooked. I loved it. I was zipping around the mountain in no time, with a new confidence I'd never experienced on skis. I was taking small jumps, skiing backwards (a little) and smiling the whole time. It was like rollerblading on snow.

Well, within a month, my daughter, my son, my husband and five of my friends had retired their skis and poles and were on skiboards! Anyway, once we tried these, our skis and poles have been gathering dust, as none of us picked them up again for the rest of the season. We have found that longtime skiers who have been skiing since they were children (now in their 40s) are vehemently opposed to these new skis and insist it is not really skiing. We say they are just jealous they aren't having as much fun as us!

I'm a 40-year-old (very) active woman. I have been roller-blading several miles a week for years and I am now taking figure skating lessons. My family (a husband, 13-year-old daughter and 10-year-old son) rented a house in Vermont the past two years and spend many weeks and weekends skiboarding throughout the winter. I am passionate about the sport.

Chris, from Holicong, Pennsylvania writes in:

My first time skiboarding was amazing! I caught on to it right when I hit the slopes and was doing jumps and skiing backwards by the end of the night! I will never go back to my skis because the skiboards are so easy to control in powder, moguls, just everything! All my friends were so jealous on the hard trails and moguls because I could just glide through like nothing and hit all the jumps, while they were struggling!

Alexis from London, England comments:

To say that I am hooked on skiboarding (Europeans, annoyingly call it SnowBlading) would be a huge understatement. Whilst my skiing had room for improvement, progress was not exactly rapid. With my 'Blades', I can skiboard down difficult slopes that I could only dream of before. The small size of these things makes carving so much easier. When I ski with my regular skiing buddy (we used to be of the same skiing standard), I find that he still has the edge for top speed when going down a very long smooth run, but at the first sign of a drop I leave him miles behind. Even jumps are so easy with skiboards.

My husband and I just moved from Hawaii to Seattle last March. I was born and raised in Hawaii so this past winter was my first 'real' winter experience. I heard about Ski-boarding (or Snowblading) through a friend of mine, who heard about this sport through her friend. Well, her friend raved about it! He said his sister who has never done any type of snow sport picked it up rather quickly. That made me think that I could do it too!

Sandra from Seattle, Washington adds:

Now, I need to mention that I had NEVER been in snow, played in snow, seen snow up and personal before my Skiboarding experience. My husband on the other hand was born and raised in Illinois and practically grew up on skis! I've got to admit, it was a little tricky (more like scary) for me at first, but once I got the hand of it, well, let me just say, we were on the slopes for almost 7 hours!

I am fully looking forward to this next season and to purchase our first pair of Skiboards! (We rented the pair we used last year). Can you imagine? ME, with my own pair of snow related equipment? Something I don't think I could've imagined just 2 years ago! I LOVE the sport! Trust me, if I can do it, ANYBODY can!

Becky from Bowling Green, Kentucky writes:

I am 32 years old and have been skiing off-and-on since I was 10. Last year, I visited Sugar Mountain in N. Carolina with a friend. Because she was a beginner, she thought renting skiboards might be a better way to go than 'those long skis'. So I rented a pair too. At first, I had to adapt to the difference in balancing on skiboards as opposed to standard skis. By mid-afternoon, I was hooked!

This season, I visited a number of websites to read up on ski-board reviews and decided that because they were such a bargain, I'd buy a pair instead of renting again. I bought the SnowJam 75 cm and skied at Snowshoe, W. Virginia last weekend. It was great! I was much more confident on ski-boards than 'long' skis and it's so much easier to maneuver (no poles!) and to get back up (on that rare occasion that you fall). I'm very happy with my purchase and look forward to skiing on them again and again.

Jeff, a snowboarder from Superior, Colorado states:

Last year I was threatening a friend that I was going to try skiboards, even though I am a good snowboarder (going on 15 years). We headed up to Berthoud Pass Ski Area in Colorado (mostly backcountry). I strapped on a pair of skiboards and we headed up the chairlift. When I first got off the chair, I thought the skiboards to be a little squirrelly, but as I got better at using the edges (after about 50 yards), they felt okay. We went down an intermediate groomed run for our first run and about half way down, I started feeling real confident. On the chairlift again, we talked about how easy it was to pick this sport up. Our second run was down a double black diamond and I had fun. We stayed on expert runs for the rest of the day.

Let me say this: skiboarding is easy to learn. For an inter-mediate snowboarder, who isn't advancing as fast as they want, because of lack of mountaintime, this will be a great thing to try. You'll be an expert by noon! It's much easier to learn than skiing or snowboarding (I skied for 10 years before snowboarding). *For inline skaters, you'll learn even faster. To anyone who enjoys sliding downhill, I say try skiboarding. You won't regret it.*

Have a Blast From the Very First Day!

Riding skiboards feels totally natural and comfortable just as if our body already knows how to ride them. Being in control, without the fear factor of skis and snowboards, they allow for more spontaneous enjoyment of the mountain experience right from the very first day. This is by far the most common comment, that skiboards are really fun to ride. Usually with skis and snowboards it takes years to get to the point that we can have fun the entire day. Not so with skiboards.

Right from the first day, we can have a great time and it just gets better and better from there. *Pure Fun from Day One* is the motto I came up with to describe this experience. This is really the experience that got me, pure fun, without inhibition. This is what launched this business originally. It only takes one day of riding them to know.

Here is what a few customers have to say.

Kellee from Idaho Falls, Idaho states:

I will never go back to long skis! I just had to write and tell you I loved skiboards from the first day I tried them. I'm a 30 some-thing mother of four and hadn't skied for 12 years. I was teaching my two oldest and tried the skiboards. Now I will never go back to 'long skis'. I wish I could have taught my kids on skiboards, it is so much easier. This year they will get skiboards for Christmas, not skis. Thanks for bringing the fun back!

Marc from Fair Lawn, New Jersey writes in:

What it comes down to is that there is no better snow sport than skiboarding. I started this year and I love it. Before I ski-boarded, I skied which I also found to be awesome, but skiing with two short snowboard-shape skiboards on your feet is beyond awesome. Even though I'm still learning on skiboards, I'm starting to get some grabs down. Now if you're a skier and you switch over to skiboards its going to feel weird for like twenty minutes of skiing, but then after that you're going to have a blast. Skiboarding is the best thing out there so when the next ski season comes around trade in your board or skis for skiboards.

Marcia, a mother of four, from New York writes in:

While on a ski vacation at Mt. Ascutney in Vermont a few years ago, we had the opportunity to demo some skiboards. The whole family fell in love with them! I just learned to ski six years ago and have done OK, but always ski on the cautious side. Having a bad knee always kept me looking at the harder slopes, but too chicken to adventure down, worrying about not being able to turn sufficiently and keep control.

When I started out this past season, I swapped back and forth between my new skiboards and my skis. On New Year's Eve, I decided to go strictly skiboards. I don't think I will ever go back to my skis again! What a blast! We live ten minutes from a local mountain and I became obsessed with coming home from work and hitting the slopes! My confidence level skyrocketed and I found myself doing slopes I would never go near on skis! The ability to turn quickly and the stability kept me on my feet doing runs I never dreamed I could do.

One evening, my 21-year-old daughter went with me (she was using skis) and after an hour she asked if we could switch. After one run she was hooked! Of course there I was on the skis back to my old cautious self again. Needless to say, I recently bought another pair of skiboards for her to use next season. I don't want to be stuck without mine again!

As I mentioned before, my son also has a pair of skiboards. He has been an avid and kamikaze skier since he was 12 - the no fear kind of kid. This past season he also had the opportunity to hit the slopes frequently on his skiboards and has the same comment: 'I have no interest in ever using my skis again!'

Like everyone else's reviews I've read, there are many questions and comments on lifts and in lines. I tell everyone what a blast they are and how they have taken me from a so-so skier to a person obsessed! Thanks so much to whoever came up with the idea of skiboards! I feel like a liberated woman!

Skiboards are Less Expensive!

Let's spend our money on travel and lift tickets, not equipment, travel gear and lessons. Skiboards range from about $99 US for entry level to about $450 US for the top end including bindings. Any ski boots will do (but read the guidelines on boots later on). What are the ski instructors going to do now? Think your local retail shops are going to say that skiboards are better than long skis when there is so much more profit to be made selling skis and snowboards?

Don't need to say much here. Just compare the prices of new skis or snowboards with skiboards and see for yourself. Don't forget to include the prices for new high end ski boots or snowboard boots compared to less expensive boots. Compare that to the more entry level boots that are great for skiboards with more comfort and easier flex. Then add in the time and money spent on lessons. You get the idea.

Dondra from Sparta, Tennessee shares:

Thank you, thank you, I dreaded to go skiing again, but I tried a pair of your $99 skiboards and am absolutely in love with them. I even impressed my boyfriend's sister so much, she's wanting to order a pair of skiboards. So cool and thanks for your site, I check it out often to see what my next pair will be, when the time comes! Watch out slopes here comes a Tennessee chick, wahooooo!

Dave shares:

Can I suggest this as another reason to get skiboards? As good skiboards are suitable for such a wide range of skill levels, from beginner to expert, provided you buy a GOOD pair to start with, you will never be restricted because you have outgrown your equipment.

Another customer states:

After a lifetime of skiing, I had grown bored, and a little dis-illusioned with the expense and effort involved in just managing the ski equipment. Skiboards gave me a freedom from all that, and after seven years of being very involved with it all, I still can't ever imagine going back to all that ski expense and effort. (Josh)

David offers:

I had my most exhilarating day on snow, in six years, on the Salomon SnowBlades. Awesome experience carving tight corners, laying out long, tight tracks of eight or twelve fast 360s, riding one-legged with great carving ability for a whole run, pushing them fast, and off the wall. After forty-eight years on those long, excruciatingly expensive skis at $1200 for skis and bindings, I'm converting to skiboards. Done Deal. Don't look back (actually, do look back, because it's so much easier to ski backwards on skiboards than skis).

Skiboards are phenomenal. I've only demoed one pair of rentals for one day and I can't wait to be out in the bumps and getting some air and having tools on my body fit for a terrain park. While I'll have to demo some, to decide on Width, Length, etc. (for the price, Hey, get Two Pair, for less than one pair of long boards), I'm gone. They are a whole different, exhilarating experience. Like being on a road bike and then discovering mountain bikes or like decaf versus double espresso.

Stay in Great Shape!

Skiboarding is the perfect exercise, because it not only is an excellent way to stay fit, but usually it's so much fun that we don't even notice the work out! Yes, exercise without realizing it is so much better than being at the gym. Hey, and what about all that fresh mountain air!

Generally, sports that involve the legs are excellent for maintaining good body tone and circulation. The right leg, especially, is often referred to by cardiologists as the second heart. Exercises that engage the legs, particularly the right leg, recirculate blood back up to the heart again. Skiboards offer great exercise for the legs.

One adventurous soul, a self-proclaimed 'Couch Potato', Sasha from Orange County, California, shares her story:

The first time I went skiboarding was in the middle of July! That's right, July. I had just moved to Colorado and all 'one' of my friends could talk about was skiboarding. We hiked to St. Mary's Glacier and skiboard down, a truly unique experience. The drive was beautiful. I'm a California girl, so I was unprepared for a REAL mountain experience. What we call mountains back home, well, I won't get into it. The vastness of the Colorado sky leaves me breathless. I don't know if it's because we're so much higher here or because the atmosphere is thinner, or what, but the sky is HUGE.

So anyway, we're driving out to the glacier and I'm craning my neck around every corner for the tiniest glimpse of snow. Finally, we saw it! As we pulled into the parking lot, we saw some hikers carrying their skis down the trail and we knew we were in the right place. We gathered our gear, clothes, and skiboards, and headed up the trail. The trail wasn't steep, but I was totally surprised by the change in altitude. Every few minutes I had to take a literal breather as my Californian lungs struggled to extract oxygen from the thin mountain air. Filled with determination, yet behind the rest of our troop, I hiked on. It took us about 25 minutes to reach the base of the glacier.

If my lungs were complaining before, they were screaming now. My muscles never even got a chance to get tired; I had to stop so often just to breathe. The higher we climbed, the more incredible the view became: snow, trees, lake, foothills and incredible clouds in the distance.

Finally, the moment of truth was upon us. I put on my skiboards and instinctively turned my tips inward, trying to recreate the snowplow ski instructors had drummed into me years ago, only to realize that it was completely unnecessary. Finally, control! In a matter of minutes, I felt like I had always been doing this. The rounded heel of my skiboards made turning easier than ever before. I experimented with my stance and found that what felt the most natural also worked the best. Never again will I pitch myself forward on a pair of skis, I vowed silently.

The snow was the worst. I am not kidding, chunky, icy, dirty snow, complete with rocks and frozen ridges. I struggled to control the chatter of my boards as I coasted over bumps and lumps. As I relaxed into my boards, I was able to control them even over this awful terrain. If skiboarding is this effortless on a glacier, I thought to myself, I can't wait until I get to do it on real, fresh snow! We reached the bottom, more exhausted from the long hike up than the too-short trip down. The glacier starts out as a green run, fades into blue, and then ends on a steep slope that I'd call comparable to a black diamond run. When we reached the bottom, we all had huge smiles plastered over our faces.

As we hiked back down the trail that had brought us to the foot of the glacier, I reflected on my experience. I came to Colorado in search of the extreme. On that day in the middle of July, I found it on the snow.

CHAPTER 3

Even More Advantages!

Following are a few more advantages that skiboards offer:

Break Out of the Conventional. Express Yourself!

You know, lessons, poles, traveling with all that equipment. Skiboards are very much under the radar with most retail store sales people clueless when you ask about them. Fun is what it's all about, not rules. Break out of the old ways and treat yourself to the experience of liberation that skiboards can provide. Be on the vanguard of something new.

Those who're often interested in trying skiboards are usually, I find, individuals who aren't driven to fit into existing social structures. They love trying new things and don't allow fear (or what others think) to stand in their way. Carl Jung calls it *individuating* or becoming your own person. Abraham Maslow calls it self-actualizing. This is that natural, inherent tendency to become the unique individual that we are.

What I find even more interesting is that many new skiboarders share that they do have to overcome the opinions of others, not to mention the resistance often met with at the ski resort rental shops. In spite of this, they follow their inner promptings and discover the secret. While conventional thought often can be a deterrent to exploring something new, be it skiboards or whatever, breaking out of these patterns helps you to step 'out of the box.'

Those who ride skiboards are not necessarily rebels, but that probably doesn't hurt. They are however self-motivated and independent thinkers who do not often succumb to the status quo. Even if this doesn't describe you, try skiboards and before long you'll begin to break through previously unconscious boundaries and experience greater self-expression and enjoyment in life. I'll be discussing this more in depth shortly.

This is really a totally new sport, operating under the radar and wide open for individual creative expression. Do you enjoy 'big air' and styling on tricks no one has ever seen before? Ever thought of dancing on the snow? Yes, with skiboards you can snow dance alone or with someone else – backwards, forwards, turning, disco! Anything goes.

Breaking out of conventional thinking regarding how we should ride the slopes, we can all continue to spark our natural playful instincts. Experimenting, trying new things, seeing what is truly possible and exploring our limits, that is what skiboarding is about. I personally was truly amazed when I discovered that riding through the moguls backwards was now possible.

Scott from Framingham, Massachusetts shares his testimonial:

After nearly twenty years of being a reluctant skier, skiboarding has converted me to an addicted skiboarding nut! I used to ski because my friends did. I wasn't good at it and really didn't even like it. I never really felt like I was in control and I certainly couldn't claim to be having fun. After a while I just stopped going.

This January we returned to Zermatt. The three of us that went last time and another friend that went on this trip. I was determined this time to ski more and like it better. Rather than rent skis however, I rented Snowblades. I ended up trying them the first day out. It was instant love! I skied them on blue trails and a few reds [advanced].

I had a great time and decided to research the available products and get a pair when I got home. Besides being a blast to ride, skiboards had another big appeal: no poles! Because of being lightweight, there is nothing to unweighting the skis to turn, so unless you want them for moral support, poles aren't needed. This meant two less things for me to carry around. In Zermatt, that's a big deal. We were being 'manly' or something so we always walked to the lifts and back, usually with ample Apres Ski at the Papperla Pub on our way back. Those little light skis with no poles were the envy of everyone on the way back at night, perhaps more so than on the slopes during the day!

When I got back home, I started looking for skiboards locally. Not having much luck, I turned to the web. Fortunately, my search landed me at skiboards.com. I read the reviews and articles, looked over the various models, and exchanged emails. They advised me on a few possible matches. I wanted something I could ski anywhere on the mountain and start to try some basic tricks on. I'm 37 and not interested in flips or anything too dangerous but riding fakie, spinning, reasonable jumps and bumps and playing in the half-pipe all interest me. I wanted to ski on New England's ice and groomed, packed trails, but also be able to ski in powder.

Randy from Falconer, New York offers this:

If you don't try these, you're missing out on something great. Several years ago my friends had been urging me to join our school's ski club, though for the first couple years I turned them down. Finally I woke up and decided to join. We went to quite a small resort where we were only able to rent skis or snow-boards. Without even hearing of skiboards yet, I decided to start on skis. It took me a couple of weeks to get the hang of it, though I looked pitiful going down the hill.

After that first year, I already got sick of skiing and was ready for a new challenge – Skiboards. I had seen a few others cruising around on them and I knew I had to try them out for myself. By that time I was in a high school ski club. We went to a larger resort that rented skis and snowboards and skiboards. What held me back from getting skiboards, was my friends. They kept telling me that I would be terrible and I would just be holding them back because they would have to wait for me. Ha! They did keep me from trying it for a couple weeks, but I was determined and eventually I got a chance to try it.

While waiting in the rental line, all I heard about was how terrible I was going to do. I showed them. On my very first run I bombed the hill and beat them all to the bottom. From that time on I was to be a dedicated skiboarder for life. Don't let your friends hold you back. You should try skiboards especially if it feels like something could be missing when you are hitting the slopes on your skis.

Accelerated Skill Development

Whether planning to ride skiboards mostly or just using them to improve your overall ski skills, these are the perfect tool for skill improvement. My own experience from the beginning days, as well as that of many others, is that the learning progression is exponential. In other words, ski skills develop super fast. Most skiboarders find that they jump levels quickly, from green to blue, blue to black and black to double black.

Each time, it's better than the last time. Imagine being outdoors, on soft white stuff, just blazing down the mountain in total control, doing whatever strikes your fancy without the hindrance of cumbersome equipment. Every day brings all new possibilities.

Here is what one person had to say:

I will never return to skis. I have skied for years, but I got the urge from seeing an ad at a ski shop. I rented skiboards for the first time and skied four days straight on them. What a rush! Blue became green and blacks became blues and I was having fun like I had never had. When I got home from the mountain I sold my skis and poles and bought a new set of skiboards never to return to skis. I am sold! (John)

Alicia, from Denver, Colorado has a great story:

How Do I Love Skiboarding? I can't believe how easy these things are. Wow! What a day. How do I love skiboarding? Let me count the ways: tremendous, awesome, exhilarating, remarkable, and I could go on and on. Piercing blue skies, gorgeous mountains, a bit of snow and, oh yeah, some skiboards all made for my glorious first time skiboarding experience. These people who have been bragging about the sport really know what they're talking about. So, now I will join the many who have shared their first time skiboarding experiences.

Okay, I'll admit it. I wasn't exactly fond of the sport on my first run at Loveland Resort in Colorado. I was having a bit of trouble getting my skiboarding groove on. After a few runs, some slips and flips (just kidding), I finally made it down the run, an hour later. My second time down was better and then by my third time down, I was a pro, well almost! By my fourth run I was tearing up in the eyes from the exhilarating ride down the mountain. What a feeling!

It was like I was being magically mentally taught on my way up the ski lift because the difference in my skiboarding between my first and second run was colossal. I went from a ninny on the snow who fell four times and took an hour to get down a slope, to a fearless thrill seeking skiboarding fanatic who never fell again.

Amazing. I haven't even been to a ski resort before. I have never skied or snowboarded. Suddenly I was riding down the mountain like I had been skiing for years. I had to laugh at the people who would literally stop in their tracks to check out what the heck I was doing. Little did they know that in a matter of a few hours, I was skiing just as well as they were.

Quite an accomplishment, if I do say so myself, considering I did a nosedive the second I got off the ski lift the first time, not a great start! But, I definitely had a happy ending, for I have fallen in love with skiboarding. Heck, this whole skiboarding thing is a million times easier than dating, and a lot more fun too. I had the time of my life! I can't wait till we hit the slopes again.

Skiboards Are Great for All Ages

No matter what age, skiboards have something to offer. Young kids up to older adults all love the convenience of skiboards. When I first got my kids on skiboards, I was relieved to not have to carry poles, long skis and all their other stuff to the mountain. Skiboards are so light and easy to carry, my kids even carried their own equipment.

People from five to eighty years old and beyond can ride skiboards. While kids certainly enjoy the fun factor of skiboards, adults embrace skiboards as well. Older adults choose to buy and use skiboards because they're easier on tight muscles, and being lighter, put less torque on the knees. They also reduce or eliminate fear. Many say it makes them truly feel young again with a whole new exciting activity to enjoy.

This was a cool testimonial from Jim of Pennsylvania:

Early last week I took delivery of my Snowjam 75's and on Sunday, I had the opportunity to try them. I will turn 58 in a month and have been skiing on and off since my introduction to the sport in my mid-thirties. With my late start in skiing and infrequent participation, I never did advance beyond novice level, and thought I would be relegated to those green and blue runs forever.

All of that changed on that Sunday at Spring Mountain in Eastern Pennsylvania, where the two youngest of my three daughters and I discovered this thing called a terrain park. My daughters are quite new to skiing and still apprehensive about anything new or challenging, and they were on conventional skis. When they saw what I could do with the skiboards, they relaxed and became much more bold just from watching me have such a good time. The skiboards improved their skiing, and they never even had them on!

I felt a little bit awkward at first, but balance came quickly and was followed by a tremendous feeling of freedom on the slopes. I could maneuver much more easily and quickly, making small corrections here and there that I couldn't think of doing on skis. Jumps and turns were no problem. I wish I got these earlier in the season. I have to say the three of us had a blast. Thanks again to Doc and the rest of you at Skiboards.com for getting me started on this.

Keith (from Park City, UT) writes in:

I bought a pair of 90 cm Salomon ski blades. I'm now a convert and have thrown away my skis! As a sixty year old with some arthritis, these are the best thing for getting mobile when long skis are too hard to turn.

Dave, from Lincoln, Nebraska says:

Skiboarding is the real deal. I have been skiboarding now for four years and LOVE it. I was an OK skier, but have progressed to an excellent skiboarder because they are so easy to use. I spend my days roaming the less traveled diamonds and double diamonds hitting untouched powder while my friends who insisted on skiing eek their way down greens and blues.

I am a youth pastor and have taken high school students skiing who have never been and at the end of the FIRST day several of them had conquered black diamond hills unharmed. Go try that on skis and snowboards! They all had fun.

On a recent staff retreat to the mountains I talked a coworker into trying them. He has been a skier his entire life and after the first day he commented, 'I'll never go back to skiing, these things (skiboards) are awesome.'

Another customer comments:

One of the appeals of skiboarding to me was not having to work as hard, while at the same time riding at a whole new level, or several levels above what I was at formerly. All the changes we seem to be making allow us to ride as older riders, with less stress, with greater maneuverability, cut deeper more radical carves, while raising our fun factor and our technical skills in all terrain. (Fred)

Skiboarding is a Fun Social Bonding Activity

Skiboarding can be a really great social activity to be enjoyed with friends and family. The great thing about skiboards is that everyone gets good quick, so all can cruise together regardless of skill levels. Everyone can go anywhere on the mountain and have real fun together. Imagine not having to wait any longer for those friends on snowboards or skis to get down the mountain! Get them on skiboards and everyone can ride together.

It's always fun to experience a new adventure together. Even if some of them are more experienced skiers, skiboards, I find, are the great equalizer. Parents can ride with their kids and have a great bonding experience (which speaking as a parent is truly always memorable). What a first date! It's even a great corporate team building activity.

One of the comments that I hear over and over from customers is how strangers just come up to them on the slopes or start conversations regarding skiboards. This is a great icebreaker for making new friends! Skiboarders regularly get swamped with questions: What are they? What are they like? Where can you get them? Are they hard to ride? I have heard of customers literally getting surrounded by people inquiring about them.

Vacationers also enjoy skiboards because they don't have to spend valuable vacation time in lessons, instead having fun right away. This way they can enjoy more time with friends and family.

Dan from Columbus, Ohio shares:

You guys were 100% right on the mark about the sport. I had never skied before and my wife had only skied twice before, over 20 years ago. After just one, half hour, lesson we were off the bunny hill and on to the big slopes. The entire experience was totally exhilarating. At the end of our first weekend, we couldn't help but chuckle while we watched other beginners who started learning, on traditional skies and snowboards, at the same time as us. They were still struggling with snowplowing down the bunny hill while we were carving up the intermediate runs on our new ski boards. Everywhere we skied this winter we managed to get at least one traditional skier to try ski boards and all of them said they would never go back! It's easy and addicting!

However the best part for us wasn't the fun, it was the fun we had with our kids. I want to tell every parent out there (no matter what their age) that it doesn't matter if their kids skiboard, snowboard or ski, we finally have a sport that you can do as a family and keep up with the kids. It was amazing, last winter our television was off and the family was out on the slopes, having a ball together.

From Turoa, New Zealand, Heather writes:

I learned to ski at age 48. My children advised 'Big Feet' and I loved them. [Big Feet skiboards made by Kneissl] I ski 70 days per year, always on Big feet, but last year I 'graduated' to some 90 cm skiboards. Still having fun. All our Grandchildren have learned on skiboards too!

Explore Previously Inaccessible Terrain

Glades, moguls, double black terrain, parks, pipes, deep powder, and backcountry, riding behind a snowmobile, kite-skiboarding, cruising on frozen lakes – it's all suddenly available to play on. Skiboards open up the whole mountain experience as the limitations due to longer equipment disappear. Since turning, stopping and controlling our speed is easy, any advanced terrain becomes possible to ride.

Most people think that because they're short, that we can't do as much on them. Wrong! The opposite is true. We can even go places on them that few skiers or snowboarders would dare to ride, like super tight, steep trees. With the ability to turn fast, the whole mountain opens up.

A skiboarder shares:

Riding skiboards has forever changed the way I will look at skiing and the mountains. I can never go back to my old perceptions. The change was so dramatic, if you told me it would be like this when I started riding skiboards, I would have seriously doubted it. (Vicky)

Sonya offers her experience:

The first busy day at Wolf Creek, CO! My friend and I were in line for Treasure Lift. Smiles radiated from our face and our skiboards radiated in the sun. As we inched our way up to the lift, nothing could top the thrill we long awaited, downhill skiboarding through the trees. We discussed our plan to go right at the top. It was then that everyone got a laugh at our expense when someone bolstered aloud, 'Someone sold you only half skis!' The crowd laughed, as my friend and I were scooped up by the lift chair, with smiles still on our faces. 'See you on the flats!' we yelled in triumph.

It was later that day when we headed adventurously towards Alberta [an advanced lift with black and double black terrain]. We made our way through the trees whooping and hollering with joy and eventually hit the flats. 'Whose laughing now?' I said to my friend as we skated deftly by snowboarders who were carrying their boards. 'Only half a mile to go!' we hollered as we left them in our ski dust!

I am sold and hooked on skiboards. As an avid roller blader and ex-skier I have found my medium of choice and eagerly take the remarks thrown my way at the lifts or on the slopes. Skiboards are versatile and the possibilities are endless! Forever grateful.

Fritz, a mountain climber shares his first time experience on skiboards:

I had only skied twice in the last ten years before buying my first pair of skiboards. My interest was piqued since I'd moved to Colorado and had seen a mention of skiboards in a rock-climber's magazine. Since I enjoy backcountry climbing, and could easily see these things as useful gizmos for descending from winter climbs, I invested.

I was quite pleased to discover that my plastic mountaineering boots would work with the bindings saving me the expense of ski boots! My first time out was at Eldora Ski Resort, near Boulder, Colorado. It was during a snap of below zero degrees, so I was bundled up like an Everest climber on summit day. The season was still young, a few days before Christmas, so there weren't too many people on the slopes. However, the people who were there did look at me funny. At least one said, 'Hey, look at those things!'

It was a blast! My previously feeble skills seemed more than a match for all, but the most challenging territory. My relatively soft boots felt more like inline skates than a ski boot would have. When I knew it wouldn't torque my already screwed-up knees, I was hooked!

As the season went on I bought a more aggressive set of skiboards, spent more time on bigger mountains, and milked powder out of the trees until April. This year I have a season pass and plan to spend all of my time on skiboards. Let the yahoos play in the terrain park, I'll be off in the rough!

Living to Our Full Potential

Hey, I say, why not master skiing, and improve the overall quality of life at the same time? To me what truly matters, beyond just being a great skier, is learning how to realize what we're really capable of in life. This is the deeper motivation for why people ski or do any sport when we get right down to it.

We all want to realize our greater potential. This is what brings tears to people's eyes and makes them scream out loud when they see an athlete excel. We watch sports to be inspired by others who are exceeding beyond the norm. It's truly exciting to watch others succeed because it speaks to our own deeper desire.

This book is more like two books in one. When I decided to write this book, I knew I didn't want to just offer my knowledge about skiboarding. I also wanted to explain what I've learned as a human potential consultant regarding the deeper connection between the art of skiing and the art of living. Fundamentally, these are the same. Skills acquired, especially those involved with breaking through limiting beliefs and behaviors, can be focused to any area of life, not just confined to the slopes. Feeling fully alive is addictive. Once igniting this on the slopes, we can have similar experiences in other areas of our life, such as career, relationships and recreational activities.

Armed with a knowledge of the fundamental principles of breaking free of conscious and unconscious limitations, our whole life can change for the better. We can transition into the ranks of the top five percent of the population called self-actualizers. These individuals express more of their potential than the average person. They live extraordinary lives.

No matter what riding level, beginner, intermediate or expert, skiboarding opens up new possibilities for self-expression, almost on a daily basis. Creative energies are allowed to flow like never before, especially because skiboards break a person out of the usual routines. Being so maneuverable, skiboards create an opening, not only by expanding our reach, but also by offering a new way of living our life as well.

The results of this new found sense of self-expression are freedom, expansion, joy, that feeling of flowing in the moment, feeling fully alive and at one with all that surrounds us. This is what's truly addictive about this sport. Peak experiences are exactly those times when everything comes together; we experience an effortlessness when riding that produces feelings of oneness, complete connection with the environment and of course, spontaneous, ecstatic joy in the moment.

Here is one description from a customer I find particularly inspiring:

The experience is a timeless, expanded space, with a heightened alertness and oneness with everything. I would call it cosmic consciousness because you're totally tuned in. It's pure spontaneity with no forethought to what actions you're going to take once the process begins. It almost lives on its own. Always different, unique, ever changing, yet familiar some-how. It always feel new, fresh, each run being like the first time. To me it's just an enveloping feeling of 'Yeah'! You want to throw your arms up and go 'Yes.' (Brad)

While all skiers and boarders experience the Zone (another word for peak moments), that experience is usually only reserved for the upper echelon, those who are good enough to really experience it on a consistent basis. Skiboarding turns this all around. Skiboards, due to their short learning curve, and the freedom and creativity that emerges very quickly, allow an easy entry into experiencing peak moments.

I'll save this explanation regarding personal transformation and self-actualization and it's relationship to your experience on the mountain for later. There's a definite direct connection between the two that I feel is the most exciting advantage regarding skiboarding. Before reading that section however, I think it's important to directly experience riding skiboards, that is, if you haven't already. Get the taste. Then what I'll be talking about may resonate more with you.

People choose to ride skiboards for many of reasons, as outlined above. Skiboarding offers numerous benefits for those willing to be open to trying something new. A fairly large percentage of our customers are simply looking for an alternative, as they've gotten bored or frustrated with traditional ski equipment. Others have discovered that skiboarding is not just an alternative to skiing or snowboarding, but is a unique sport in its own right. Other customers want to have fun right from their beginning days. As skiboards don't break the budget, many customers who simply don't go to the mountains enough to justify the expense of getting outfitted with a ski package (and lessons), choose skiboards instead. What a great bonding activity with family and friends to all go experience something fun together. No matter what the reason, overall, skiboarding is a whole new adventure and something definitely worth experiencing in life!

CHAPTER 4

Skiboards: The Equipment

People tell me that there's more to life than skiboarding.
Well, of course, I know that. It's just that
I can't really remember what that was.

Choosing the Right Skiboards

My company, the Skiboards Superstore, has always spent a huge amount of time researching prospective skiboard products. I, and my employees, ride them, hear from customers who ride them, and work with the manufacturers, so we can continually communicate the performance characteristics of our products. We know how they perform in all different conditions and terrain. It's with this background that I offer the following information to help you select the right skiboards.

When choosing skiboards, there are a number of factors to consider. In selecting skiboards, we want to choose based on construction and design, performance characteristics, and what conditions and terrain they're intended for, as well as price, and of course, graphics. At the same time, remember that any skiboards will be fun in a variety of conditions, so it's not quite so critical that you choose just the perfect pair.

For those who've had the chance to ride skiboards, they know that all skiboards are fun and way easier to learn to ride than long skis. Skiboarding is great no matter what age, ability level or personal riding preferences. Everyone is up and riding on skiboards in a few runs or one day at the most, and from then on, the fun really begins. This is true no matter what skiboards you're riding.

So this means, any skiboards are a good choice. You can't really go wrong with anything you buy. However, since there is a wide variety of skiboards based on size, price range, brand, construction and overall performance, it can seem overwhelming at first when shopping for skiboards. Therefore, I want to elaborate on some of the essential factors to be considered.

Skiboards – The Quick Selection Method

Any skiboards that you select are going to be a blast right away and offer a much shorter learning curve than skis. Consider this the quick selection method, find a pair that you like the look of, at a price you want to pay, buy them and start having fun. You won't regret it. They're all great!

Skiboards – The Specific Selection Method

For those a bit more particular about finding a pair of skiboards that are more specifically suited to your own personal style and preferences, here are some additional factors to consider. From my personal experience, as well as talking with thousands and thousands of customers since the early days of 1997, consider the following:

Height and Weight

It's important that you feel your skiboards will handle your height and weight. Most skiboards are intended for those 59 inches and above in height and variety of weight ranges. Skiboards, not being like skis, don't require certain sizes for a particular height and weight. What a relief that is!

Note: We do carry skiboards for those under 59 inches. You can find these in our Just for Kids section.

Some skiboarders swear by shorter skiboards (75 cm or under) even though they may be 6 foot tall. Kids and adults use these boards and can totally advance to extreme skiboarding on them. Yet, others may feel more comfortable on longer skiboards. If unsure, a general range of 75 cm to 99 cm is a safe bet for all around, all mountain, riding and quick fun from the first day.

Performance

Choosing the right skiboards depends a lot on what you want to do on them – this is one of the most important factors. Do you want to jam through moguls, get air and land some outrageous tricks, cruise the half pipes, lay out carves on the groomed runs, dance down the slopes turning 360s and one-foot turns, go through the trees or just carve some turns and have a great time? Do you want to explore extreme terrain, float in deep powder, go into the backcountry or just do all of it (all-mountain skiboards)?

Shorter skiboards are more maneuverable, easier to learn on, great in moguls, glades and have the feel of inline skates. However, they may not handle those long, deep, lay-it-over carves at speed and don't have the surface area for smoother landings in the parks. Shorter (but wider) shorter skiboards ride great in powder, but not quite as well as the longer, wider ones (like the 99 cm).

Longer skiboards offer more speed and allow for the deeper, shoulder-to-the-ground carves. Big air addicts usually go with longer boards because of the extra speed and surface area for landing tricks. If you like tricks (on the ground and in the air), a symmetrical twin-tip design is also recommended.

Of course, construction of the skiboards also contributes to performance. Higher quality construction, such as laminated wood cores, triaxial fiberglass layers, rubber dampening, even aluminum reinforcement plates for greater retention of release bindings, yields higher performance and dependability. Sintered bases are faster and hold wax better, though extruded bases (a little less expensive) are quite durable and fast, but don't hold wax as well. It's mostly true though that you get what you pay for.

Binding Choice

Another factor to consider is binding preference. Some skiboards come with release bindings, others only with non-release and a few with both options. In addition, if you choose to use snowboard bindings, choose skiboards with the 4 hole mounting pattern. These options are clearly marked in the product descriptions.

Just starting out?

For something to learn on, do a Shop By Brand on Skiboards.com and check out these models:

Summit Headwall 95 cm

Summit Jade 87 cm
Snowjam (75 cm and 90 cm)

Head Salamander 94 cm

Matrix 75 cm, 90 cm or 99 cm

Atomic ETL 123 cm

Elan Freeline 99 cm

Just starting out, but love going big and riding aggressively?

Love getting air and landing awesome jumps? Jamming down the slopes and laying out some awesome carves? Choose skiboards that deliver the speed and have the surface area for landings. First, a twin-tip design is better for riding both forwards or backwards. This particular design features front and back tips that curve up, so it's easier to land tricks backwards as well, or be able to turn 360s on the ground and add some overall flair to your riding.

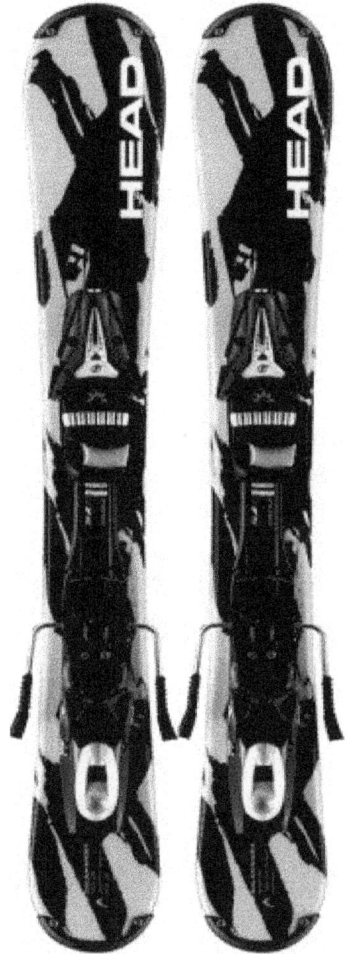

On the narrower side (feel more like a combination of skis and inline skates) look at:

Atomic ETL 123 cm

Elan Freeride 99 cm, 125 cm and 135 cm

Snowjam 99 cm

Summit Freedom 99 cm

Snowjam Park 125 cm

Summit Headwall 95 cm

Head Salamander 94 cm

These models will handle more like skis, but with the advantages of skiboards. These are also the easiest for skiers to transition into, with the quick edge-to-edge responsiveness that they're used to. You can ride them with boots close together.

On the wider side, with greater width at the tips, tails and waist, the following skiboards will perform more like a combination of skis and snowboards. These wider skiboards allow more drag-your-hand-on-the-ground carves, better landing surface for getting air, higher speed (you'll be surprised at how fast you can go) and greater stability, not to mention cruising powder better than the narrower ones. Consider these:

Snowjam 75 cm and 90 cm

Summit Jade 87 cm

Summit Nomad 99 cm

Summit Custom 110 cm

Summit Marauder 125 cm

The wider the skiboard design, the more it carves like snow-boards (getting them on edge). Wider will easily handle conditions like powder, crud, altering snow conditions and offer more landing surface for jumps.

Want true All-Mountain skiboards?

Do you like cruising the entire mountain, like the glades, moguls, groomed runs, pipes and parks, powder and backcountry, all of it? Then consider the following:

Snowjam 90 cm

Summit Nomad 99 cm

Summit Custom 110 cm

Summit Marauder 125 cm

Atomic 123 cm

Elan Freeline 125 cm

Icelantic Scout 143 cm

Of course, some skiboarders would include other products we carry in this section, so it's truly a matter of personal preference. I always have a few pairs in my trunk depending on my mood. I do sometimes have trouble deciding which pair to ride though and can be seen at the resort staring into my trunk from time to time.

Backcountry Anyone?

Skiboards are great in the backcountry (off trail). They pack light and you can either boot pack (climb in your boots) or snowshoe up the hill with ski boots in the bindings. You can also mount them with AT Bindings, such as the Fritschi Diamir Freeride bindings and then add skins for climbing.

AT bindings (all terrain) provide rock solid performance on the mountain, release in case of a fall and rival any alpine release bindings on the market. However, they also offer the advantage, with the flip of a lever (you don't have to take your boots out of the bindings), to free the heel for climbing uphill. This is especially useful in the backcountry for ascents and then you can lock them for downhill riding. These bindings also come in handy on traverses and going back up the mountain at your local resort instead of riding all the way down to the lift. These special all terrain bindings come with a higher price, however due to the number of high tech features.

In addition, for climbing with AT bindings, you'll want to add climbing skins to your skiboards that are easy to put on and off. These allow you to glide forward without slipping backwards. This way you can just glide uphill on your skiboards, take the skins off at the top, tighten down your bindings and down you go. No lift tickets!

For backcountry, consider the following skiboards:

Summit Nomad 99 cm

Summit Custom 110 cm

Summit Marauder 125 cm

Icelantic Scout 143 cm

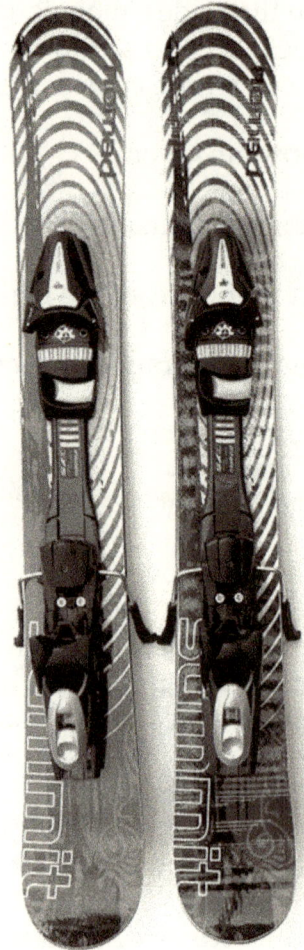

Upgrading From Last Season?

Since by now you're a confirmed fun-addict, most likely you know what you're looking for. You probably have a good feel for what you want and reading through the descriptions and specs should help. You can also call our experienced staff for personal recommendations based on your specific needs.

Consider top-of-the-line high performance skiboards and bindings, however. At this point, get the best. You can keep your old pair for friends to try. Email us at: info@skiboards.com for more specific advice.

How About for Kids?

For those under 59 inches, the Snowjam 75 cm, Matrix 75 cm or other kid's skiboards work best (featured on skiboards.com). Some kids like the Head 94 cm or Summit Headwall 95 cm also, but it depends on their height. Either way, let your kids have fun instead of torturing them on those long skis. They'll take to it much faster and won't want to go to the lodge or go home half way through the day.

For younger kids just learning, consider the RC ski harness as it makes it easier on you and allows them to have the freedom of turning (while you can check their speed). See our *Just for Kids* section on the website.

What about Snow Dancing?

There really is such a thing with fancy footwork and even couples dancing. Check out our ski dancing video in our Video Clips section posted by two ballroom dancers who are riding skiboards. Maybe their outfits might look outdated, but they sure do add a whole new dimension to what is possible on the slopes!

To ski dance, look for skiboards with the most skate-like feel. It's quite fun to dance down the slopes with a partner or more (some even go down with three to five friends). Skiboards make this possible. If you're interested in experimenting with this style of riding, choose shorter, more maneuverable skiboards such as the:

Matrix 75 cm

Summit Headwall 95 cm

Summit Jade 87 cm

Snowjam 75 cm

Head Salamander 94 cm

Conclusion

Ultimately, any skiboards are fun. It usually just comes down to personal taste in graphics, design and of course, price. Make sure to check out the reviews on specific skiboards posted on our website or talk with one of our experienced skiboarders to discuss your options.

Also consider two other options: Take advantage of our Rental By Mail program to try before you buy. We offer many skiboard models that you can rent by the day and return when you're done. Also, check out our Skiboards Outlet to find less expensive models or demos for sale.

Always, of course, feel free to email us at: info@skiboards.com or call us toll free at 800-784-0540 (U.S. & Canada) or International at +970-884-2947.

CHAPTER 5

Additional Skiboarding Equipment

Skiboard Boots

All regular ski boots fit skiboard bindings, whether they're the release or non-release type of bindings. What is important about ski boots though is that they're comfortable. With skiboards, the stance is upright. More aggressive boots often create a forward lean that can create undue pressure on your thighs as you try to stand upright.

Therefore, the less expensive boots, such as a beginner or more intermediate level boot are best. We do make it a point to choose boots at the Skiboards Superstore that will work best with skiboards, so you can always feel confident of the boots we sell.

It's handy to have rubber tread on the bottoms of the boots for ease of walking to and from the slopes. Hard plastic bottoms on boots are quite slippery, in contrast. Micro-adjust buckles are handy as they allow the exact right fit.

For the best fit in a ski boot, when you're standing up (or leaning slightly back), while wearing your ski socks, there should be about one-half inch to one-quarter inch distance from the big toe to the front of the boot. Again, comfortable when standing in your boots is key. In other words, they should fit like a comfortable pair of hiking shoes or sneakers.

Consider an insole other than what often comes with the boot. A custom insole with built in arch supports will allow you to get just the right leverage when carving. Insoles allow you to get better contact and edging control. This means that as you lean, there is more direct power transfer to your skiboards and edges.

This is especially true for those who have pronation or fallen arches. The best way to improve this problem is to get a custom orthotic, where they make a cast of your feet. These can be pricey, but will make a huge difference. If you don't want to spend the money on this, then just find a store-bought insole that feels right to you, such as Super feet, Power step, or even Dr. Scholl's. Just make sure they are not too soft.

Skiboard Bindings:

There are essentially three types of bindings that can be used with skiboards. Two of these bindings fit ski boots and offer their own unique advantages, while one fits only snowboard boots.

1) Non-Release Bindings

The sport of skiboarding began with the use of non-release type bindings. Non-release bindings don't come off when you fall. You're required to use leashes so they don't get away from you and speed down the slopes should they become detached from your boots. When you fall, it's kind of like falling on a pair of skates. You just get up and go again. You don't have to put your boots back into the bindings or chase them down the hill.

The advantage of non-release bindings is that they're often less expensive and provide great 'road feel', meaning you have a direct connection with the boots, bindings and ground. However, with these bindings, if you get in a tight spot, they won't release, so there's an increased chance of injury. **There are currently no regulations in the ski industry prohibiting the use of non-release bindings, however.**

Another advantage of non-release bindings is that besides fitting regular ski boots, these bindings can sometimes fit hard shell snowboard boots, AT boots and even telemark boots. Sometimes they'll also fit mountain climbing boots.

Most high performance non-release type bindings fit 4-hole stainless steel inserts installed in the skiboards during manufacturing. This mounting pattern is in a standard 40 mm X

40 mm square pattern usually towards the center or sometimes slightly back from the center point. These bindings adjust by hand, Allen wrench or screwdriver.

Certain non-release bindings, usually of a more composite construction, are drilled directly into the skiboards. These most often are mounted with eight screws. These adjust easily, mostly by hand, and work just fine, providing a lower cost alternative. However, they may inhibit flex somewhat.

Adjusting Non-release Bindings to Ski Boots

All non-release bindings work the same. There is a heel bale (metal wire) and a toe bale (metal wire with toe lever). First thing to do is adjust the bindings so they fit your ski boots securely. Adjusting the binding to fit your boots is often either a turn of the dial, or screw adjustments to move the toe and heel bales forward or back. Make sure the fit is tight, yet not so tight that you can't unclip the toe lever when needed.

At the mountain, to put on your skiboards with non-release bindings, follow these steps:

1. Make sure the bindings are adjusted to your boots before arriving at the ski resort if possible.
2. Scrape all the snow off the bottom of your boots. If not, the bindings may come off when riding as the snow falls away.
3. Put the back lip of your ski boot into the back metal bale until it's secure. Make sure your boot is all the way back.
4. Lower your ski boot on the binding so it's flat. Take the toe clip in hand – rest the bottom of the toe clip on the front lip of your boot and snap the toe lever over your boot.
5. Note: the toe clip needs to secure the boot so the boot does not move side to side, yet still be able to be removed without too much effort. Sometimes there may be some adjustment necessary to make sure the toe lever fits securely.
6. Take the leash attached to each binding, wrap around

boot or leg and make sure it's attached. Leashes makes sure your skiboards won't get away from you. This requirement is true for snowboard bindings and telemark bindings at the resort as well.

Tip: On an incline, place your skiboards on a glove, so they don't slip from underneath you when getting into them.

2) Release Bindings

While it's always been true that the majority of skiboards have featured non-release bindings, the understanding was that they were so short, it was easy to maneuver out of potentially hazardous situations. Because skiboards are not as long as skis, there would be less force placed on legs and knees in a fall. As well, as this has been predominantly a crossover tool for skaters, most skaters being used to falling and just getting back up, skiboards provided a remarkably similar feel.

Over many seasons, talk began about adding release bindings to skiboards. The problem has always been that standard ski-type release bindings were too long and cumbersome to mount on these. Many skiboarders at first were concerned about prerelease of the bindings, particularly when in potentially dangerous situations, such as in the air or riding through the trees.

It used to be that release bindings often weighed more than non-release bindings also. It also used to be true that release bindings sometimes impeded the flex of skiboards. Things have changed since the early days of skiboards however. As ski binding manufacturers make it their job to allow the full flex of skiboards (or skis), while also delivering maximum 'road feel', there is little difference these days between the performance of release and non-release bindings. These do not prerelease (when adjusted properly) as some had feared.

Still true however is that most ski-type release bindings, due to providing extra safety features, add to the price of skiboards. I think it is still overall much cheaper than a trip to the emergency room!

Release bindings in my experience are much more popular. The primary reason is that when mounted on skiboards, these create one of the safest snow riding tools on the mountain. Then, there is the added convenience of step-in-and-go bindings. You don't need to bend over to put them on and you no longer need leashes, as the bindings come with brakes (acceptable at the ski resorts) that usually keep your skiboards from escaping down the hill. All of this contributes to the popularity of release bindings mounted on skiboards. I repeat, nothing else really compares to the safety of skiboards with release bindings on the mountain (other than sitting in the lodge).

Most release bindings offered at Skiboards.com are adjustable to a full range of boot sizes. However, you can also use regular ski release bindings that fit your specific size ski boot. For example, you can take the bindings off your existing skis (make sure these are tested by a shop though) or buy new ones from local ski shops or from us. Once adjusted, either way, you're ready to hit the slopes, after you set the DIN, that is.

More about the DIN: The DIN or *Deutsches Institut für Norman* issues the standards for alpine ski binding settings. The correct DIN setting is based on height, weight, ski boot sole length and ability level of the skier (cautious, average or aggressive) and age (if 50 years or older). The DIN setting allows the alpine bindings to release when a certain amount of torque is applied, as in the case of a falling skier, thereby protecting the rider. The DIN setting needs to be set by a certified ski tech to make sure the bindings are adjusted correctly and that they won't malfunction. (Reference: Wikipedia.org)

Adjusting Release Bindings to Your Ski Boots

Assuming you have adjustable release bindings, usually there is a color chart or markings on the bindings with ranges of boot millimeter sizings. Find the size on your boot (it's usually found on the heel, for example '298 mm') and find the right adjustment range on the bindings. Move the toe lever and heel lever (usually a release lever needs to be moved first) to the correct settings. Once set, then take your boot, make sure the brakes are in the down position and put your boot into the binding making sure it fits properly. You don't want any sloppy movements of your boot in the binding. If in question, as you're getting your DIN set at a local ski shop, have them adjust your bindings to your boots.

At the mountain, to put on your skiboards with release bindings, follow these steps:

1. Scrape any snow off the bottom of your boots first.
2. Put the toe of your boot in first and push all the way to the front under the binding.
3. Bring down the back of the boot until the brake lever goes up and noticeably clicks into place. This locks your boots into the bindings.
4. Once you do this for both bindings, you're ready to play. Simple!

Tip: To get out of your bindings, you push down on the heel lever, your brakes snap down and you're out.

Warning: There have been some after market release bindings that fit the 4-hole skiboard mounting pattern. These are often on risers. These are not adequately tested nor endorsed by any major binding manufacturer. They may not release when they need to. In addition, these may not provide the maximum carving performance or necessary road feel. Be cautious when considering buying any bindings that are not the recognizable brands of the major binding companies in their approved formats and current models.

For those who may have older skiboards with non-release bindings, these can sometimes be custom fitted for release bindings. Visit our Pro Shop at Skiboards.com for more information.

3) Snowboard Bindings

Many Summit Skiboards as well as some other brands come with standard 40 mm X 40 mm stainless steel inserts that will also fit standard snowboard bindings. However, as snowboard bindings are wider, they'll tend to catch when carving unless they're raised a little. Skiboards.com now offers an adaptor kit that gives the necessary rise under the snowboard bindings. This allows you to mount regular snowboard bindings and be able to use snowboard boots with your skiboards.

One thing to keep in mind is that skiboards are carved by putting your weight to the sides of your boots and bindings. The stiffer the sides of the snowboard bindings and boots, the better they will be for carving. Besides the common two buckles, an extra retention strap higher up on the binding will also help to provide better carving ability.

However, many advanced riders also use the back tails to carve on skiboards discussed later. If you're of this persuasion, snowboard bindings can be used more easily because snowboard bindings have stiff backs.

Using snowboard boots adds a whole new dimension to the sport of skiboarding. Comfort, ease of hiking and walking and easy conversion for those who already snowboard are some great advantages for mounting snowboard bindings. This is a great combination, given the possible limitations of side-to-side carving (binding dependent). This is a leading edge in the sport and will no doubt be evolving in the years to come.
Stay tuned.

Poles?

The majority of skiboarders choose to ride without poles, as poles are not necessary to pick your turns as with skis. Poles can get in the way. About the only time they may come in handy is at the lift or on the flat spots. Often, for those times, telescopic adjustable poles can be used. These poles can then be stashed in a backpack when riding down the slopes, so your hands are free.

I usually recommend starting out using skiboards without poles. This allows you to get the proper centered position and let you experience the sense of freedom that skiboards offer. In addition, it focuses attention on your feet, which is where it needs to be, especially at first.

Ski poles, especially if you used them before with for long skis, have a tendency also to put you in a forward lean position out of habit, taking you off center. However, if you're comfortable with using ski poles already, use them. Just don't do the forward lean thing.

Carry Bags

A skiboard specific carrying bag is handy. You can use it for travel or in the back of your trunk to keep your boards protected so they don't bang together. Skiboards.com offers high end, padded, carry bags that have room for gloves, extra socks, tools, and more. They are made with internal cinch straps to keep your skiboards secure as well as carry handles. These are offered in a variety of sizes to accommodate all size skiboards. If you're traveling, I feel these are essential and they do fit in the overhead bin of most planes. They come in 100 cm, 125 cm as well as in other sizes up to 145 cm.

Other Typical Equipment

As with any snow sport, for proper clothing, layering is best. There is no official clothing for skiboarding – wear what is comfortable. I would recommend high tech ski or snowboard socks, such as Lorpen socks for maximum comfort and better performance, however. Warm toes are definitely important.

I do strongly suggest a helmet for safety and comfort. Not that you're crazy, but there are others that are. I first decided to use a helmet when I got hit in the head with skis that someone was carrying over their shoulders outside the lodge. You never know and keeping your brain intact is a very good thing.

The other advantages of helmets are that they keep your noggin warm and they can be bought with built in speakers to attach an mp3, iPod or smart phone. You can use the speakers and wiring for talking on your phone when necessary, without having to remove your helmet.

PART II

Instant Skiing

Let me see, it's easy to learn, is totally fun from the first day, it opens up the entire mountain for your creative pleasure, is less expensive than typical snow riding equipment and you don't need lessons because it feels totally natural! I'm thinking it will be around for a while, even if it never becomes a mainstream sport. Instead, I believe it will achieve the status of a cult sport, with worldwide enthusiasts who were fortunate enough to have discovered the secret.
- Doc Roberts -
(Response to an interview question: "Will the Sport Last?")

CHAPTER 6

Awakening Our Natural Instincts

Imagine turning when we want! Just think about stopping and we stop! Have places on the mountain that elicit fear? Not anymore. Once feeling the confidence that skiboards inspire, we'll have to rethink what Intermediate, Advanced or even Expert signs mean.

With the ability to balance and turn easily on skiboards, skiing becomes wonderfully effortless and instinctual, whether using traditional ski techniques or trying new creative ideas on the mountain. Now, anything can be done with less stress, effort and anxiety, as compared to long skis. When it feels more like skating on snow, new possibilities can emerge.

In contrast, steeper terrain, combined with long skis that don't turn very quickly, and are quite clunky in comparison, makes for a challenging and fearful combination. Peak experiences are rare in these situations. Instant skiing or rapid improvement is nonexistent. It's just plain not fun and the lodge starts to look much more appealing after a few runs.

It's no surprise to say that it takes longer to learn to ski on long skis than to learn to ski on skiboards. It would even be faster to learn to ride long skis when starting out riding skiboards first! This is true even for seasoned skiers, as skiboards promote proper balance and weighting. Many skiers find their skills improved when giving skiboards a try for a while.

The main point about instant skiing, whatever we're riding, is that we need to be totally comfortable and in control of the equipment. Once this occurs, we're then able to ride the slope without thinking about the equipment anymore. Becoming one with our skis, now they're more like an extension of our bodies.

This is what frees us to simply enjoy the totality of the experience and let go fully into the moment.

Breathe in the beauty and joy naturally inherent in gliding through the snow in a winter wonderland. These are the moments when snow riding becomes truly exhilarating. This is why we go to the mountain. This is why being a good skier is so important. The faster we learn, the better. It's exactly why we don't want to waste our precious time stuck in lessons!

Can any of us remember our first attempts to stand and walk as a baby? Maybe not. Just watch a baby take their first steps sometime. While a little wobbly at first, they just get it after perhaps a few falls. Their natural physiological instincts kick in. The innate ability to learn, balance, take forward movements and navigate the terrain take over. Of course, they're not in their heads with all the tips, suggestions and instructions of how to learn to walk either.

This is the miraculous human physiology at work. It knows what to do if given the freedom to do so. What is true is that our body already knows how to get in the flow. Just like a baby learning to walk, it's this very innocent experience that forms the basis for moments of immediate joy and effortlessness on the slopes. Being fully in tune with the moment, fully present in our bodies, the core experience of joy can naturally arise within us. Joy is not after all a mental experience or idea, but is an actual physical feeling.

The real magic on the slopes happens when our innate instinctive response takes over. As this occurs, we're able to learn to ride the equipment much faster, relax and be more in our body. Attention is now free to focus where it needs to, rather than being caught in thoughts of confusion, analysis or resistance. Awakening our natural instincts, greater freedom dawns and our skills improve.

As one customer relates to this:

There is always a sense that something that was being held inside me gets released during that time. (Chris)

We all possess the natural instincts to ride skiboards or even skis. Instant skiing only requires the right knowledge and equipment. The balance, the intuitive feel of turning, the ease in stopping, feeling comfortable even on difficult terrain, all can emerge quite naturally. The more we're able to get back in touch with our own inherent wisdom to move and navigate the terrain, the faster the learning curve becomes.

Allowing our deeper instincts to lead the way requires at first a simple refocus. It means creating an internal bypass to all the ideas, fears and 'how to's' gleaned from either ski instructors, well-meaning friends or even our own conditioned self-doubts. Reawakening the spontaneous capacity we knew when younger is simpler than stuffing our heads with details, facts and what if's. We already possess the instincts to move, groove and flow within our bodies, just like when we first learned to walk. Now it's a matter of releasing it.

While I'll be offering suggestions and tips on various riding styles with skiboards, please understand that this is not a how-to book in the typical sense. These suggestions are more about learning to focus attention intentionally to discover our own inner wisdom. It's not about technique, but about getting back in touch with our body awareness and intuition. Once the body awareness is re-stimulated, our instincts awakened, riding with greater confidence and ease will flow naturally.

Instinctual Learning

To embrace the art of instant skiing requires reorienting our approach to learning. Most learning in our culture uses the left part of the brain. Left brain learning focuses our attention on analysis, logic, reason, research and planning. The left brain is about study, comparison, future rewards and essentially controlling circumstances to be able to succeed. These are all valuable abilities for sure, but in our culture they overshadow instinctual learning, which has taken a back seat (if accessible at all).

Left brain training is the prime approach in our mainstream educational systems. This is the dominant approach in ski schools as well. Often based on years of research to understand intellectually what works best, techniques are taught to control and manage the equipment. Over time, with much repetition and memorization, we usually understand and incorporate the techniques that allow us to progress in our abilities (yeah)!

As well, traditional ski training programs usually focus to only learning to master the equipment. What they teach is the latest thinking on how to control and maneuver those long skis with hopefully some grace, of course adapted to the latest and greatest ski innovations. The equipment recommended in the rental shops however is usually based on height, no matter what the ability level. Length becomes almost another means of subtle control because lessons now become mandatory.

I am shocked that shorter lengths are rarely, if ever, considered as a possibility for ski schools. As some customers have shared, arguments occurred with rental shop clerks and ski instructors when they wanted to try something shorter (or much shorter in the case of skiboards). Sharon, a skiboarder from England writes:

I've struggled for five years skiing in Europe, trying to use traditional skis (150 cm) and having god knows how many lessons from a variety of instructors in each resort. I told my husband that the feeling of fear and panic when I took the slopes (blue ones at that) was now so bad that I didn't want to go skiing again. Two weeks ago a new indoor snowdome opened an hour's drive away, and I plucked up the courage to try the new skiboards that were available.

One of the ski instructors there did everything he could to discourage me, saying they were 'girly' and not 'proper' skis! He said he could get me to ski where others had failed. I stuck to my guns, thanked him and put the blades on. Wow, for the first time ever I have felt what it is like to ski. I cannot believe that after 5 years of fear, panic, anxiety, and being tense from head to toe, it vanished in 5 minutes. I have been back since, to make sure it wasn't a fluke, and can now race my husband and son to the bottom of the slope without so much as a wobble!

I can't think why one of those instructors seeing how distressed I was, didn't suggest them rather than lose me from the slopes altogether.

Awkward, at best, learning to stop as well as turn long planks can prove quite difficult at times. "Be sure not to cross the ski tips!" That may not be so easy when there's all that length in front of your boots. No matter what, even if on the slopes weekly (or daily), it takes years to get good enough to experience frequent peak moments. Looking graceful is often totally out of the question. Usually, for the majority of skiers, intermediate runs are more of a lifetime sentence.

What traditional skiing translates into is usually more lessons, more frustration and more of our life stuck in the same old habits. This long learning process makes it harder to get to the goodies, which is the whole point of wanting to ski initially. Long skis just plain don't offer the same natural feel as skiboards do. It takes time, effort and money to learn to manage and enjoy long skis.

Another customer states:

I remember one of the reasons I switched to begin with was because my skiing skill became somewhat stagnant after two seasons of skiing. I didn't enjoy skiing because of that steep learning curve. Now, after almost four seasons of skiboarding, I can go down the black slopes with my regular skis and do it with a lot more style! (Shelly)

One more thing I want to say about traditional skiing. Having the skills just to ski right and portray the correct image doesn't necessarily mean we get to experience the feelings of pure joy and exhilaration that we'd expect. Skiing that is only mechanical, where we must follow the prescribed rules and apply all the correct techniques, will not bring true joy on the slopes (which personally I feel is the main point).

If truly committed to learning to ski instantly, and have instant fun at the same time, besides using skiboards, another learning approach will prove a helpful addition. In contrast to the left brain learning approach, the right brain orientation is intuitive, creative, spontaneous, flowing and elicits a natural connectedness between body and environment. Learning from right brain is about here-and-now, in the very moment, tuned in to what is happening and reacting from that centered place. It's body oriented rather than head oriented. This is the domain of instant learning, when our natural instincts can fully engage.

Listen for a moment when skiing (or during some other active sports) to the thoughts flowing through the mind. As we tune in, we can become aware of a steady stream of instructions, self-criticism, fears, worries, doubts, confusions and all manner of chatter. This inner voice is busy firing directions and skewed motivations to motivate us to do it right so that we can avoid fear.

Don't take it personal, it's a cultural phenomena. Left brain learning is perfect for our culture of control. To control or manage change in an orderly fashion, we've learned to compartmentalize, scrutinize, dissect and direct our attention into methods that will provide order and security amidst the seeming chaos. Feelings, instincts, intuitions, soul-inspirations and flowing with change aren't really encouraged.

As children, we easily mastered new skills without much intervention. Like riding a bike, learning to skate, playing video games, children usually learn faster than adults. There's a natural openness and ease with which we're able to learn something new when younger. Right brain or instinctual learning happens effortlessly for children.

Children simply trust their bodies to adapt quickly. Learning for them comes with a sense of excitement and freshness of appreciation, as they rejoice in the physical movement. It's totally natural. Life is full with breakthroughs and peak experiences as a result. This is right brain learning in action.

I would like to share with you the following article from Mark, a skiboarder and one who 'unschools' his kids. *Unschooling* is a name given to allowing the natural desire to learn to emerge from within a child, rather than being imposed by teachers from the outside. As a result, kids are just guided from within to allow their innate talents to shine forth and they naturally align with their true creative potential.

Unschooling on the Slopes

I've never skied. I've never had the desire. I grew up in Southern California and never really got to know snow, or what a fun combination snow and gravity can be. Furthermore, money has always been tight – I thought the stereotypical Southern California skier runs off in his BMW to his Mammoth condo – and I always thought I couldn't afford the equipment, the lift tickets, not to mention the condo or the BMW! Besides, learning to ski seemed hard, not something where one can have fun the first weekend.

This last winter several things happened: Our friend told us about all the fun they have skiing in the mountains above their house, how cheap it can be, and how much easier the new parabolic 'shape' skis are. My daughter caught ski fever from talking to my friend's kid. She made it sound like just another form of unschooling (she has a way of doing that).

Also, I came across an article on skiboards that are not only great fun, but easy to learn. That's the right combination for me! I looked up the things on the Web and started getting excited.

My daughter and I arranged for a long weekend. I called and found a pair of skiboards. We borrowed some pants and stuff, and off we went. My wife made us both promise that we would take ski lessons so we wouldn't do anything stupid like meet our death skiing while out of control crashing into a tree when playing football!

We met our friends and went up to Sierra Summit. Once dressed and strapped into our skis (skiboards), our friends took off up the mountain with their skis and boards. My daughter and I went to the bunny hill. We had two hours to kill before ski school so we just went up and down the bunny hill, trying this, trying that, talking about what worked, watching others and trying what they did, falling down, getting up, trying again – basically, playing.

By the time ski school started, we looked at each other, shrugged, and got on the main lift. We had taught ourselves to ski, and didn't want to sit through the basics again. We didn't need ski school – we had unschooled ourselves!

The rest of our two days on the slopes we continued our self-education process, trying one thing and another, talking about it on the lift back up, and trying again. We were both awed by the beauty of new snow in the forest.

We got better and better. We were able to take runs a little faster, try harder runs, gracefully carving instead of shuddering our way down just barely in control. We stopped falling (well, pretty much).

Skiboards allowed me to learn fast, and fall less. That's the secret to having fun, right? This is an intense be-here-now experience that you can learn to do in a day. Skiboards let me learn to turn fast, control my slide, and carve slopes that I would never have been able to try in the first weekend on skis or a snowboard.

Am I an expert? Hell no. I can handle blue runs, and I expect that a few more days of skiboarding will let me take on black runs, all while having fun and being safe.

The weekend was one of the best examples of home schooling

I've experienced: A combination of challenge, a desire to learn, with experts to watch and being able to experiment in a supportive environment. Best of all, it was FUN! At ages 46 and 9, we unschooled ourselves into confident skiers. Next winter you'll find us in the snow, wearing big grins while experiencing the reality of Newtonian physics!

This is a great example of what I've been sharing. We can teach ourselves by just attending to what is happening in our bodies, in the here-and-now moment. While we're having fun, we're also breaking through previous conditioning and outdated habit patterns to tap into our innate wisdom. A whole new adventure dawns.

It's the thrill of being in the moment, not knowing what to do next that is the real high, no matter what the snow riding equipment. It's exhausting and even nonsensical to believe using our left brain will guide us towards having this experience. Instead, the left brain creates a disconnect between our body and our mind and removes us from the moment-to-moment experience. Instant fun in contrast is in the letting go, surrendering to pure freedom. This does not happen when believing we can control all the circumstances by simply trying harder.

Instinctual learning or unschooling is about flowing, experiencing increasing moments of effortlessness and being in a state of childlike discovery and fun. The faster we can shift into these flow states, the faster we improve our ski skills and the more joy we can experience. There is quite an extensive body of research that supports this approach. Our capacity to have a great, liberating, ecstatic day on the slopes from the first day and every day after depends on this primary instinctual capacity to let go and play.

Reawakening our instincts, our body wisdom, we're more capable of tuning into and learning to ride the equipment faster. This happens when we no longer have to think about how to turn, stop or deal with varying terrain. Flow experiences or peak moments of joy occur precisely when we're no longer needing to figure out how to use the equipment and get down the mountain.

Heather from Chester Springs, Pennsylvania writes in:

I have to say, I tried skiboards this past winter and I just fell in love. I had only tried skiing once (the day before I tried skiboards) and I just hated that. I must say skiboarding is much easier and it feels more natural.

With age, our natural ability to learn becomes overshadowed by repetitive patterns of thought and behavior that systematically and increasingly interfere with these primal instincts. Left brain learning patterns begin to dominate early in life. This disconnects us from our natural instincts and the essential core of our being.

To truly free our capacity for instinctual, right brain learning, understanding how early conditioning subtly sabotages this is essential. With this knowledge, it becomes much easier to recognize outdated, restrictive and unconscious habit patterns as they surface. As a result, letting go into the moment and reawakening our natural spontaneity is liberated.

These fundamental principles of breakthrough psychology are quite relevant to learning to ski instantly, but the bonus is that it also assists us in creating whatever else we may want in life. In the next chapter, I'll briefly review the powerful cultural conditioning that early on subverts our Authentic Self and therefore our innate capacity to blossom into our full potential. While I take a slight diversion from discussing skiboards, I believe this is relevant to the target of instant skiing and instant fun. References will be provided in case something triggers your interest. These references are included at the end of the book.

CHAPTER 7

Paradigm Shifting

Our concern must be to live while we're alive – to release our inner selves from the spiritual death that comes with living behind a facade designed to conform to external definitions of who and what we are. Every individual human being born on this earth has the capacity to become a unique and special person unlike any who has ever existed before or will ever exist again. To the extent that we become captives of culturally defined role expectations and behaviors and stereotypes, not ourselves – we block our capacity for self-actualization.
- Dr. Kubler-Ross -

My lifelong quest has been to discover the catalyst that would enable each of us to live to our full potentials. I remember, as a child, being intimately familiar with this unrestricted, almost limitless feeling of sheer delight with life. There was a flow of endless play and all its creative possibilities. As the years passed however, as I look back, I realize as so many others do, that the seeming magical feeling of sheer joy and flow as a child had somehow faded. We of course can rationalize this, but the fact remains.

I have always loved this poem by William Wordsworth because it truly captures the essence of this loss of freedom:

Heaven lies about us in our infancy!
Shades of the prison-house begin to close
Upon the growing Boy,
But he beholds the light, and whence it flows,
He sees it in his joy;
The Youth, who daily farther from the east
Must travel, still is Nature's priest,
And by the vision splendid
Is on his way attended;

At length the Man perceives it die away,
And fade into the light of common day.
- William Wordsworth -

As Wordsworth so eloquently points out, the walls of the "prison-house" close about the growing child and the clarity and vividness of perception once experienced, slowly disappears "into the light of common day." While once knowing unbounded joy and beholding the "splendid vision" as children, somehow this experience becomes imprisoned in the world of the ordinary. Unbounded joy and all its creative possibilities simply fade away. Along with this, that natural ability to learn easily and effortlessly seems to disappear along with it.

Driven by my own desire to live to my own potential and inspire the same feeling of play and joy I knew as a child in others, I really wanted to understand the cause of this loss. Over a couple of decades of research later, I found the answers. Particularly the knowledge stored within the fields of neurophysiology and breakthrough psychology are applicable in explaining what obstructs us from realizing our true potentials. On a fundamental level, whether it's learning to ski better, or be healthier, or get better grades or make more money, the same principles apply.

The human physiology learns at a truly amazing speed. It takes very little time for learning to occur when our body takes the lead. As certain behaviors are learned, they turn into automatic and unconscious habits. No longer needing to keep relearning that particular behavior, we're able to continually move on to learning new things.

Remember for a moment first learning to drive a car. It was all so fresh and new and even overwhelming in the beginning days. Over time, however, we adapt and it soon becomes automatic. Driving a car today, most of us don't even remember how we got to our destination. Of course, and this is important, this physiological learning process does not discriminate. It keeps learning, keeps adapting to any circumstances, but also even the unwelcome ones.

Paradigm Paralysis

Thomas Kuhn first coined the term *paradigm* in his book, *The Structure of Scientific Revolutions*. A paradigm is defined as a framework of thought or belief that explains a particular aspect of reality. Paradigms provide us with road maps, a way to view our world that aids us in understanding and operating in our lives.

Starting out as a simple theory or way to understand life, particular paradigms soon evolve into the overriding filter for our perceptions, determining how we'll interpret our life experiences, as well as react to them. This worldview can affect everything: the way we interpret our experiences, how we behave, interact with others, form our self-concept, choose life goals and values, and even what and how we think. While originally paradigms provide a structure with which to organize and understand our world, they eventually obstruct new, more expansive and less conventional ways of living our life.

Simply put, as we're conditioned to accept the dominant cultural paradigm, our ability to stay open to new possibilities in life fades. Operating from these fundamental assumptions, our perception begins to discriminate and eventually block other possible viewpoints (occurring on a physiological level as well). This state of early adaptation to these cultural paradigms is often equated to falling into a *consensus trance* (Tart), or becoming *inauthentic* (Shoham) or *mindless* (Langer). I refer to it as *paradigm paralysis*.

There is a powerful dampening effect that cultural conditioning exerts over us. Succumbing to the particular worldview or mindset has a way of placing limitations on who we are and who we can become. In many ways, the outcome is that our spirits are dampened, creativity is thwarted, appreciation of life is obscured and our capacity to acquire new skills is limited to the existing and acceptable means of learning.

Life becomes structured in predictable ways according to these underlying paradigms. What happens during our life is often based on those expectations that have been predetermined by our culture. (Bruner; McClelland and Liberman; Solley and Murphy) In other words, we mostly experience what we (or what others or the culture) expect us to experience. Talk about a dampening effect on our spirit!

A paradigm acts like a shield, protecting us from what could happen. While our cultural paradigms are quite intertwined and pervasive, one in particular I feel is of relevance to our discussion. Control, a predominant worldview in our culture, gives us a sense of security and attempts to create a firm footing from which we can better interpret and deal with what is happening in our world and personal lives. It has long been believed that maintaining control will give us the means to prevent our society from falling into chaos. Fundamentally, this worldview appeals to our basic need for survival in a hostile universe!

Not surprising, fear plays an instrumental role in the belief that control is necessary. The news stations for example cater primarily to fear. Potential threats to our survival get our attention. They also boost network ratings. The focus is usually on what horrible catastrophes could happen, and so we pay attention to these possible dangers and work to avoid them. Playing on our fears definitely contributes to keeping us in line.

Instrumental to the control paradigm is establishing a topdown social structure. Rules and systems are in place to assure everything runs smoothly and that order is maintained. The belief is that without authority figures enforcing the rules, our society would fall into utter chaos and none of us would survive. Essential to maintain this top down system is learning respect for those perceived to be in authority.

Social control is of course a necessity for many reasons. Obviously, for example, there would be way too many car accidents without people obeying street light signals. Aligning with this cultural paradigm and the fear response is part of the process of becoming civilized. It allows us to all get along. Yet, of course there is a cost.

This dominant mindset of control is best served by operating from the left brain (reason, logic, facts, and analysis). Rational is good, while feelings are considered irrelevant. In contrast to the left brain, the right brain is about connection, spontaneity, intuition and flow. Right brain functioning has been systematically played down in our culture of control. After all, inspiration, feelings, spiritual connection and natural instincts are not real easy to control. They're also a little too close to the feeling of fear.

Emphasis on left brain thinking has become the predominant focus of attention in our culture. Thinking proves an effective way to rehearse this focus to control and thereby internalize it. Cultural conditioning then continues to subtly reinforce those thought patterns that are consistent with this predetermined mindset, while other, less conventional thoughts, are filtered out or censored entirely. (Fromm; Kabat-Zinn; Jaynes; Koestler; Krishnamurti; Ouspensky; Pearce; Quarrick; Tart; Watts) What results is that from an early age, we learn how and what to think. Particular patterns of thought become habit, while other possibilities are excluded from our attention (often for life).

It is these conditioned thought patterns (particularly clustered around the need to control and avoid fear) that prevent a direct experience of the moment, of what is real and thereby obstruct instinctual learning and creativity. The normal process of thinking, "Is not, by itself, open to the discovery of anything new, for its only novelties are simply rearrangements of old words and ideas." (Watts) As long as we're engaged in thought, we're under the direct influence of the forces of automatization and mindlessness. (Hartmann; Jaynes; McClintock; Seligman; Sperry) Quite early, we learn to adopt these acceptable thought patterns, believing them to be the only way of viewing our world.

Another aspect of the control paradigm is an orientation towards the future. Subtly convinced that working hard and putting off until tomorrow, we believe we'll get the socially acceptable rewards we so deserve. Someday we'll be happy, that is, if we keep working, continue striving and hoping. Keep in mind that what we believe will make us happy, is of course also defined by our culture.

The cultural emphasis on control predetermines how we'll react to situations in life, like learning a new sport. Once indoctrinated, our physiological adaptation response assures that we'll simply act according to our previous habits, with little actual personal control over our actions, since it generally operates on auto pilot. (Jaynes; Pratto; Solomons) It's probably not surprising that the common human tendency is to act or react (as well as think) along these well-worn habitual pathways. Translated, this is why welcoming something new like skiboards (or snowboards when they first appeared) is often difficult for many people. It rattles their cage.

So, as a result of early cultural conditioning, and the amazing physiological adaptation process, specific patterns of thought, perception and behavior become automated. We then become in essence paralyzed by these culturally determined habit patterns, such as controlling and being controlled, that are continually working behind the scenes, totally invisible and extremely powerful. The pure flow, the aliveness and joy we may have once known as a child has often faded as a direct result. Consequently, it becomes harder to be open to and learn new things as easily.

Let's now briefly take a look at how this process of conditioning is instilled.

The Human Commodity

We are all hypnotized from infancy. We do not
perceive ourselves and the world about us as they are,
but as we have been persuaded to see them.
- Harmon -

The control paradigm demands fitting into the existing social structure. We're all subjected to this conditioning process. Gaining the approval of others, particularly those in authority, establishes the social order and allows us to understand what guidelines and rules are acceptable. Fitting in gives us a sense of security and reassurance that we'll be happy in life.

The process of cultural conditioning begins with our parents (who pass on their own conditioned beliefs and patterns). Teachers, relatives and all manner of authority figures join in to promote the cultural agenda. This training is delivered by powerful others who use emotional as well as physical force, along with the rewards of love and approval, to harvest appropriate habits. Abraham Maslow, psychologist and researcher, describes it this way:

> *Since others are so important and vital for the helpless baby and child, fear of losing them (as providers of safety, food, love, respect, etc.) is a primal, terrifying danger. Therefore, the child, faced with a difficult choice between his own delight experiences [urge to self-actualize, to be fully alive, experience peak moments] and the experience of approval from others, must generally choose approval from others.*

Growing up, we're taught to behave. Constant messages like: 'pay attention,' 'don't make noise,' 'obey,' 'don't cause trouble,' 'listen,' 'stay still,' and more, bombard us. This is all subtle training, fed by the cultural mindset, to make submitting to control a priority.

The early educational system reinforces this overall belief that we're being constantly watched, monitored and graded and expected to measure up. Very subtle it is, to be conditioned to believe that if we follow directions, listen to our elders, work hard, put in the effort and play by the rules, we'll all succeed and be rewarded someday. These are all forms of control at work, subtly using fear of punishment as the negative motivation.

Our lives become one of striving to fit in, projecting the right image and acquiring all those things that we've been taught we should have to be happy. "Nearly every human activity has some standard against which performance can be graded." (Quarrick) Life becomes preoccupied with seeking and achieving, rather than finding, happiness. As a culture, we live on hope that one day we'll make the grade and get our just payoff. Hope, by the way, is a powerful tool for maintaining control.

The media manipulates this paradigm of control to promote their own agenda and further embed this conditioning. Through all manner of advertising, the message that is delivered repeatedly is: To be truly happy, feel more alive and successful, we must achieve a certain level of status, recognition as well as the correct image.

This *attention engineering* is quite sophisticated. Cultural conditioning and the existing paradigms are well understood by these *engineers*. (Bush) One investigator commented, " Advertisers cater effectively to mindlessness. They understand this early programming and the need for people to seek approval, to fit in and achieve success (according to the standards embedded within our cultural paradigms)." (Langer) As true masters of psychological manipulation, the media bombards us constantly from all sides, making sure we receive their message and do what it suggests.

Why have I chosen to discuss this in a book about learning to ski instantly? Besides giving some insights into why we may have lost touch with our natural instinctual learning ability, my intention is also to point out that in the process of conditioning, we have all lost something even more precious. We've lost our connection with the essential core of who we are, our Authentic Self.

As a result of this powerful early conditioning, we've learned as a culture to overrule the private flow of our own experience, instead becoming governed by verbalization, reason, social pressures, doubts and fears and the general demands of the business of living. (Quarrick) It's estimated that by the time we reach adulthood, this business of living is the dominant focus, with pure experience becoming secondary or even unavailable entirely. In everyday waking consciousness, our attention is now primarily controlled by culturally imposed mindsets hard wired into our neurophysiology. This is what a few researchers have referred to as mindlessness or consensus trance.

Shaped we are by the surrounding culture to become normal, to fit in, to selectively shape certain potentials and inhibit others.

We now manage our behaviors so they agree with consensus values and beliefs. (Tart) Little by little, our own authentic individuality becomes molded and shaped causing us to lose touch with our unique potentialities.

Being persuaded to do or acquire what we believe will bring us happiness (culturally ordained) further reinforces the paradigm of control. Unfortunately, what effectively is suppressed simultaneously in our culture is our natural, instinctual ability to self-actualize. Altschuler and Regush found that: "The Corporations, their advertising appendages, and the mass media have skillfully created consumer illusions, as our everyday cultural world has built a screen in the human mind, shielding us from our possibilities as a species." The media would have us believe for instance that self-actualizing is about acquiring more, making more money, buying the right education, proper investing or taking that next cruise.

Consequently, our own instincts, our true inner knowing, our natural ability to learn and evolve in our own direction are not acknowledged. Becoming disconnected from our inner essence, we eventually lose touch with our innate capacity to respond to the moment (an essential prerequisite for instant skiing). Over the years, we continue to practice these skills of disconnect, unaware of their consequences because, after all, it's all we know.

This business of living does not serve us, that is, if we're truly interested in being fully alive, happy, and living to our true potential. The following quotation I believe captures the essence of this fundamental dilemma:

Our obstacles to inner freedom are usually formed during childhood. As children we know how we feel about things, and we seldom hesitate to make our feelings known. But pressure from family and friends leads us to adopt the more narrow views and patterns that conform to what people expect. When our natural ideas and feelings are discouraged, we grow out of touch with our senses, and the flow of communication between our bodies and minds inhibited; we no longer know what we truly feel. As the patterns of suppression grow stronger and more fixed, our opportunities for self-expression diminish. We become so used to conforming, that as we grow older we let these patterns rule our lives; we become strangers to ourselves. (Tarthang Tulku)

Ultimately, our cultural addiction to control and profit blocks each of us from living to our unique potentials. Control in this context obstructs personal evolution. We can't really solve the problem of how to self-actualize by improving or strengthening or educating based on using more control either. The desire to realize our full human potential doesn't fit into this existing cultural paradigm (except for what the media reinterprets for us).

It's always been true that society does not get liberated, only individuals do. Csikszentmihalyi has studied this problem extensively. He concludes that the solution rests with learning to detach from external social rewards and our future orientation, instead focusing to our own intrinsic values that are within our power to embrace. Learning to attune to our body, to give attention to our instincts, to stay present and derive joy from the moment ignites a new level of personal fulfillment. Rather than putting life off until some future happiness (often tied to culturally determined goals not often of our own choosing), we can live life on our own terms (a key ingredient in self-actualization).

Truth is that when we're not preoccupied with the business of living, we can experience who we really are behind the persona. Our Authentic Self (as opposed to our Conditioned Self) emerges in these times, allowing us to excel in our own unique way. We're able to experience true joy, not what we've been led to believe will make us happy.

Letting go of our need to control (and our unconsciously belief that we need to be controlled), our right brain gains dominance, bringing in the qualities of intuition, instinct, transcending limitations, creative inspiration and a deeper union with the whole of life. I will explore this shift more in depth in the last couple of chapters.

Skiing and Paradigm Paralysis

Every time a serious attempt has been made to introduce
short skis for normal use, the entrenched orthodoxy of skiing,
let by instructors, ski makers and racers;
have pooh-poohed them off the slopes.
- Bob Parker, *Skiing Magazine* -

The ski industry is not separate from the overall culture, nor immune to the control paradigm. Fitting in, gaining approval and of course, doing what is expected are well entrenched here as well. It's no one's fault, nor is it society's fault, for its allegiance to control. This structure has been in place a long, long time.

At the ski resort, observe people wearing the latest colors, riding the newest equipment (at proper lengths), using the correct boots, and riding how they've been taught to ride. Watch a ski movie or glance through the ski magazines and you'll see attention engineering at work. This of course all keeps the consumer machine operating. Nothing wrong with this per se, as the resorts need to stay in business.

It's true of any dominant cultural paradigm that what's new meets with resistance because it threatens the status quo. (Kuhn) Any major changes are not well received and this is true within the ski culture as well. Remember snowboards when they first appeared on the ski slopes? They were black listed by many resorts. In the beginning years, snowboarders were the subject of ridicule by many skiers and the overall ski industry. Most reactions to snowboards and snowboarders were those of disapproval and criticism.

Snowboarding challenged the status quo, breaking through existing limited thinking regarding how a person is supposed to ride down the mountain. Snowboarders exposed the underlying paradigm of control adhered to by the ski related industries. This created resistance. Of course, snowboarding is now incorporated into the overall ski culture because it brings in big bucks. Notice though that they're still called 'ski' resorts.

Skiboards also introduce the element of change like snowboards did at first. They don't really fit within the existing mindset of the ski industry. There are a number of reasons for this. First, they're less expensive, so already the ski shops don't like them because of a lower profit margin. Then, skiboards don't really pay the salaries of ski instructors either, since usually most people don't need lessons and are off playing right away.

Skiboards don't really look like long skis or what you should be riding either. It's not part of how we should look at the resort. Oh my God, no poles! Perhaps the real kicker though is instant gratification! Immediate gratification is often the most threatening of all because it transcends the usual left brain learning curve, as well as the strongly embedded pattern of needing to work hard to achieve a goal.

For decades, the way to ride the mountain was using traditional long skis (at the correct length). This is what we had to learn, if we were to truly enjoy ourselves gliding on snow. Subtly everyone bought in to this mindset. If we wanted to ride the mountain, we rode long skis. Period!

Proper length of skis to ride is rarely questioned. This was all worked out for us according to a formula a long time ago! While what is considered correct length has changed over the years, it's still the formula that must be adhered to, whatever it is at the time.

Oddly, if you think about it, putting a beginner on a long pair of skis (often the same length as an intermediate or advanced skier might ride) doesn't make sense. Longer skis are harder to control, maneuver and have fun on. No problem! Take lessons and learn how to manage them and the problem is solved.

Our culture for a very long time has been about acquiring the correct status symbols – the right automobile, house, spouse, brand names, and in the case of skiing, the right ski equipment and proper skills to use them. Profit, not fun, is the primary motivation. How can control be maintained if people aren't behaving according to the rules? They can't be off self-actualizing and doing their own thing!

Is it really about the latest and greatest long skis, the biggest, slickest tricks or going steeper and deeper? Perhaps, if that is what you love, but not if that is what you believe you must get to, to be happy, cool or successful. This is where the conditioned belief begins to break down. Once we can begin to question our belief about how to ride the slopes, we open ourselves to entertaining alternatives.

I often thought as I was on the mountain in my early days of riding long skis, that other skiers were doing fine, so what was the matter with me? I'm intelligent, reasonably athletic, so what am I doing wrong? I still clearly remember those moments when my muscles felt so tight from fighting what seemed like impending death if I didn't turn just right.

The worst part of skiing for me was the constant process of trying to figure things out. I remember all those 'how to's' gained from lessons and those great tips from friends and other skiers. Then there was all the negotiating of changing conditions, terrain and weather. I spent most of my time on the slopes, in my head, analyzing and trying to figure out what to do to gain control, rather than truly enjoying the moment.

Though I'm sure it makes sense that we ski just to have a great time with our family or friends, in the great outdoors, this may not always come to fruition. Frustration with our skills or equipment, experiences of fear and doubt, or even self-imposed judgments can all interfere with us realizing the goal of being a great skier. This frustration often stems from trying to fit into the status quo inherent in the ski culture.

What I've found with skiboards is that they provide an immediate quantum leap forward in breaking free of this skiing mindset. We don't have to work hard to get our just rewards or fit in anymore. Underlying all the advantages discussed earlier inherent in riding skiboards however is the greatest advantage. The real motivation I believe for trying skiboards is because deep down we suspect that we're caught in a subtle worldview that somehow inhibits our greater freedom and joy. In this, skiboards are enticing as a new way to break free and awaken new capacities within.

When riding skiboards, or even just walking around with them at the resort, we might often feel like we don't quite fit in. So as a tool for breakthrough, I find that skiboards are the perfect way to see where our own internal programming, our cultural conditioning, paralyzes us in unconscious habits. Skiboards bring to light our inner limitations, allowing us to recognize and easily release them.

Skiboards have not gained mass acceptance like snowboards or skis. I suspect they won't ever fit into the mainstream, operating instead behind the scenes. As such, skiboards afford the continuing opportunity to break out of the pecking order, the mainstream consensus trance. Breaking free from the current view of how we're supposed to ride the slopes and what we're supposed to ride, can bring us back in touch with that sense of play and freedom we once knew as children. It allows us to see with new eyes.

Not surprisingly, skiboarders meet many skiers who can't quite relate. Quite often when telling them that they're skiboards, or ski blades or snowblades, they still can't relate. I've found that only when I call them 'short skis', do they understand. This is what fits their mental concept (even though they're really not short skis).

Skiboarders also report hearing comments like: "Did they shrink in the wash? Aren't those for beginners? Are those just for tricks? Could you only afford half a ski?" My favorite though is: "That's cheating!" Of course, there are all kinds of creative variations on these themes. This mostly comes from skiers however, as most snowboarders still remember the days when they were made fun of for not fitting in. Usually, snowboarders seem more curious than anything, especially resonating to the phrase: 'They're made like two small snowboards.'
However, many say the novelty serves as a great icebreaker. People are curious and ask how skiboards ride. They're genuinely

open to hearing about skiboards. Either way, my point is that riding skiboards will regularly solicit reactions, positive and negative, exposing unconscious thought and behavioral patterns. We don't fit and it can shake people up. They're surprised, and even sometimes shocked, by what we're doing.

I personally remember a time on the lift when a woman asked me about skiboards. I said that they're really easy and so much more fun than my skis. Her comment was, "Skiing is not about fun, it's about discipline, hard work and earning your turns." I was at first surprised by her comments. Then I understood that this was someone stuck in the control paradigm, without realizing it of course.

I do not choose to spend my precious time on the mountain (or in my life) working hard to earn my turns. As far as I'm concerned, I paid for my lift ticket and now the fun begins (and I don't care what others think). I'm here to enjoy the mountain vistas, breathe in the fresh air and have the thrill of gliding down snow while playing with gravity. I'm done with unnecessary hard work, thank you very much.

What I like about skiboards is that there are no requirements to measure up to external standards of performance. The sport itself has no acceptable image to achieve. We simply allow our natural instincts to kick in and just enjoy our time on the slopes. It's time to play, with no one to impress. What a relief that is! Whether long time skiers, first timers, skaters or dancers, we can get on skiboards and express ourselves in totally new ways.

I absolutely know from my own experience as well as from my personal research, that skiboarding is a simple way to regain the magic and joy of childhood. I hear this from customers all the time. The mountain environment is great for transcending the everyday world as it is. Then add the ability to master the equipment quickly along with the freedom of riding something that maneuvers so easily, and you've set the stage for true transformation. This is true for first timers as well as long time skiers or snowboarders.

Break free. Celebrate being alive now and cruise the slopes with total abandon. And cruise the slopes of your life equally with total abandon. Your life comes with an expiration date, so what are you waiting for? You were a child once and intimately aware of the flow of joy and magic in life. Time to rekindle that again.
- Doc Roberts -

CHAPTER 8

The Art of Letting Go

When one is engaged in a favorite pursuit or a subject
absorbingly interesting, the normal conception of labor
or time and artificial social distinctions disappear from
the mind. In fact, life itself is absorbed in the engagement,
or it may be said that one's life is now in full harmony
with eternal life.
- Koizumi, judo master -

So what does it really take to break free of paradigm paralysis and break through to realize our true potential on the slopes? It requires letting go of control, of fitting in and of old ideas, restrictive beliefs, unwarranted fears and the resistance to trying something new. I know this may sound complicated. I can almost hear: "Sure, just lobotomize my personality then!" Certainly from the above discussion of paradigms, this could seem impossible as these patterns are all so deeply engrained in our physiology and psychology. Yet, it could also be quite simple. Read on!

Being described in the quotation above by Koizumi, are moments of absorbed attention. These are special moments when we become fully engaged in the activity, in the present moment, and in full harmony with the whole experience. In these moments, mental (left brain) activity subsides and body awareness or natural instincts (right brain) take over, doing what comes easy. Once the mind shuts down, this shift becomes totally natural and effortless. This is referred to in the literature as a *paradigm shift*. During paradigm shifts, we transcend existing habitual patterns of thought and behavior and step out of embedded physiological patterns that have previously restricted us.

One rider explains it nicely:

It's a bodily experience. I become more aware of my body and what is going on internally. I take that experience and express that externally or outwardly. My mind kind of goes into a different state, it is not intellectualizing or thinking, the way I would normally think about things. It just goes into a state that is free flowing with whatever is happening. (Chris)

This rider's experience mirrors decades of research. As numerous studies demonstrate, these peak moments or paradigm shifts occur when pure experience overtakes cognitive activity. Thinking, which typically dominates our attention, particularly within a culture of control, has been found to subside during paradigm shifts. Thinking is not just a distracter, but what is even more divisive is how it acts like a barrier, fragmenting and splitting us off from our pure experience in the present moment.

Habitual thought patterns create a wedge between the experiencer and their experience. As Tom, interviewed in my dissertation states: "Thinking is always one step behind. Thinking compartmentalizes, gets us stuck, limits you, splits you off from experience. It gets us lost in hope or fear which removes us from the one-pointedness needed." As long as we attend to our thoughts, we're removed from our direct experience, clouded in abstraction, stuck in repetitive patterns and alienated from the present. (Fromm; Pearce)

So, it's interesting that ski lessons can often produce the opposite effect of what we'd expect. Going down the mountain trying to remember what to do takes us out of the moment. It obstructs the process of letting go fully into the experience. It thwarts the body's natural wisdom, instead engaging us in the habit of thinking about what we're doing.

While ski lessons can certainly teach us how to ski (given the time), the problem is that there's also a strong tendency for students to get in their heads. Learning with verbal instruction and being taught how to control our skis immediately causes us to lose body awareness. Out of sync with our body, including our posture, feet and natural rhythm, we become disconnected, as if two separate activities are going on.

Letting go, while totally natural, given the restrictions imposed by our conditioning, is something that often needs to be practiced at first. Letting go itself of course is quite easy, it's just the opposite of controlling and forcing or pushing towards a goal. In our Western culture though, this is an ability that is not usually favored, encouraged or even allowed.

I refer to letting go as an art. With art, what is essential is being able to let go or in other words, allow our creative expression to flow forth from within without restriction. We can't force art. An opening is created when the mind turns off. From deep within us, our essential nature, our gifts and our drive to realize more of the possibilities in life turns on. Letting go is not something we do, it's much easier than that because it's a relaxing of all restraints, becoming totally absorbed in the moment of play.

Based on years of research and thousands of subjects, the prerequisite conditions for the art of letting go, of becoming fully engaged in this absorbed attention experience (i.e. flow) are that the activity engaged in must: 1) be joyful to us; 2) allow us to push the limits of our abilities (move past fear); and 3) provide the opportunity for continually challenging ourselves to breakthrough to new levels of performance (room to improve).

Prerequisite 1: The activity engaged in must be joyful to us.

It makes sense that when we're enjoying an activity, it's easier to attend fully to the experience. We naturally relax and let go into the activity. Joy is the first necessary prerequisite for the art of letting go. Without even realizing it, we just slide into living in the moment, like kids at play.

The art of mastering skis or skiboards requires only a simple focused attention. This fully absorbed focus could also be described as a relaxed concentration. As attention flows to what it's interested in, the body awareness opens up and our natural instincts take over. As thoughts quiet down, we drop the need to control and our overall experience becomes one of continued joy and effortless involvement with the activity at hand.

Being quite naturally mindful to what is happening in the physical experience of skiing, our attention can easily flow from one moment to the next, focused to what is occurring right now. "When an activity is thoroughly engrossing, there is not enough attention left over to allow a person to consider either the past or the future, or any other temporarily irrelevant stimuli." (Csikszentmihalyi) It's in this letting go fully into the experience that we're most capable of reacting, negotiating the changing terrain and conditions and being present to the whole mountain experience. Our body will know what to do as we're no longer mentally distracted.

Research supports this understanding that to create paradigm shifts or breakthroughs in learning, we must attend holistically to the moment, reacting naturally, from instinct. Letting go into the experience allows mental activity to subside (without trying to do so of course). With the suspension of the rational, critical mind, the 'Flow' state or 'Zone' emerges. This experience can't be manipulated or forced. It just happens when we stop putting our attention on the 'how' and like an artist in the act of creation, we let go into the present felt experience.

Skiing, and more specifically skiboarding, offer a great opportunity to step out of the Conditioned Self and the paralysis of the control paradigms. Easily and even instantly, we can disengage from restrictive habit patterns of thought and behavior, on and off the slopes. The experience truly delivers incredible joy and liberation.

I like what one skiboarder says about this absorbed attention experience:

I lose sight of the real world that I have to operate in all the time. It just goes away. It is as if my real self comes out. It feels more like being a child. All masks and limits drop. (Jeff)

Fully absorbed in the activity of gliding down the mountain, playing with gravity, and letting go completely into the experience brings out the best in us. No games, no pretense, no rules, just having fun and grooving, fully in the present moment. All mental activity has subsided.

Take a moment to watch a bird in flight. I mean stop and really look! When the bird is riding the wind currents (not flapping their wings to get to the next current), they're playing with gravity. It's amazing to observe. Let yourself get into the feeling of it. What a great example for cruising down the slopes and playing with gravity. Birds aren't working at flowing, they're just making effortless carves without thinking (if they can think) or trying to remember how they did it the last time. Birds are in total let go and at one with the wind. They can teach us a lot about how to let go and be in flow.

Skiing can be similar, just carving this way, in flow, that way in flow, just reacting in the moment to all the constant changes happening while riding down the mountain. This is really not different from birds riding the wind currents. THE EXPERIENCE IS FLOW. It's incredibly thrilling and totally rejuvenating. Capturing the essence of this experience is a bodily experience, not a mental one. Letting go is the key to flowing and being in your body. Joy triggers this natural absorption.

Prerequisite 2: The activity must allow us to push the limits of our abilities.

To continue to break through our own limitations and culturally determined mindsets that cause us to go unconscious and into disconnect, we need to kick it up a notch. The second prerequisite for paradigm shifting into peak moments is allowing ourselves to push the limits of our abilities. Gravity and the varying mountain conditions provide this very opportunity.

Concerning getting down the run, gravity takes care of that. If we're facing down a slope, we're going down! Riding at the edge of our abilities is more about navigating our speed and direction, while being completely in the moment, in tune with the ground, physical movements and instantaneously reading all the conditions (kinesthetically). Thinking about what to do next doesn't work. Relying solely on this, we're no longer present, instead disconnected from our ability to attend to the ever changing mountain scenario.

However, testing the limits of our abilities, living on the edge, requires a total attentiveness to be able to ski, and in many cases, survive it. It's this ability to fully attend that emerges when we're pushing a little past our comfort zone. Fortunately, as we do, we tune in automatically and can let go. In effortless flow, spontaneously changing speed and direction happens much faster, a skill made much easier of course when turning something shorter like skiboards. It's this riding on the edge of our abilities that plants us fully in the present and in our bodies, where we definitely need to be.

Grooving with gravity, we transcend our usual and habitual sense of the everyday, awakening instead to an entirely fresh, fully alive adventure. This is commonly accompanied by greater expansion, effortlessness and freedom, along with an enhanced creative expression and renewed enthusiasm. It's as though everything becomes simple, clear, bright and more fluid. These are all documented characteristics of peak experiences by the way, that I'll be reviewing later.

As one rider states:

Nothing you do is out of sync. It seems so natural. Nothing else matters and I feel like I can't do anything wrong. You are aware and adjusting to what you are doing, but you are not fixated on anything. It just flows. You have to be fully present. In this state, there is nothing else, you are 100% there. You can just slide into the zone. It is an instant shift. (Jeff)

Totally absorbed in the moment, with attention focused exclusively on doing what we truly love, peak experiences are inevitable. It's precisely at these times that we breakthrough to new levels of performance and personal expression as well. This is what puts the 'instant' into skiing.

Attention is rarely one-pointed in everyday waking state of consciousness, however. Most research points to the common tendency for our attention to be fragmented, chaotic and subject to drifting from one focus to another. "Chaos, not order, is the natural state of mind. When no external stimulation engages attention, thoughts begin to drift randomly." (Csikszentmihalyi; Tart) This random drift is not so random, but moves along specific, culturally induced and automated pathways requiring no real effort. What we attend to, unless we introduce a bypass, will continue to be caught in drift, focused on the priorities engrained through cultural conditioning, not necessarily on what's best for our personal growth.

In other words, most of the time, the routines and habitual patterns of daily life keep backing us into yesterday's limitations, rather than being fully present in the here-and-now. To continue to opt for comfort, security, and familiarity keeps us locked in the habit of maintaining control, and consequently, life-stifling habits. It's very much like living our entire life in a hypnotic trance (*consensus trance* as Charles Tart terms it).

To break free of the habit of attention drift requires learning to refocus our attention in a conscious way. (Ferguson; Moore) In our culture, this skill is rarely mastered, however. Old patterns have a strong tendency to constantly pull us out of the present moment and put us back into drift (or autopilot as I like to call it). It's normally very difficult to stop thinking and talking to ourselves. Refocusing attention to the present does require a certain effort, especially at first, to break the hypnosis.

Research reveals that this automated, negative drift of attention can be overcome. "Attentional training and the cultivation of concentration are regarded as essential for overcoming the fickle wanderlust of the untrained mind." (Walsh & Vaughan) This statement suggests that retraining how we attend can circumvent the conditioned drift of consciousness. Other studies confirm the conclusion that attention can be trained and rescued from automatization and negative drift. (Csikszentmihalyi; Kabat-Zinn; Maslow; Perls; Rogers; Vaughan) It can be done.

Precisely it's in testing our limits, riding on the edge of the unknown, that provides the missing ingredient. It's in these moments that we can regain conscious control of our attention and break free. Pushing past our comfort zone engages and fully absorbs our attention. It's a survival thing! It's what creates the necessary bypass to the normal state of disconnect.

This second requirement plays a significant role in instant skiing. This is the path of totally focused attention, yet in a relaxed state of let go. There is really no effort involved, unless the muscles need to tone up. Remember the advantage of staying in shape that skiboards provide? Well, this is when that comes into play the most.

As one interviewee describes it:

It happens when I race because it's that adrenaline rush that you get when you do something right, when you do it well and you keep building on it. To get that particular experience, I have to push myself. If I do what is only comfortable for me and doesn't require any extra effort, I don't get to that same point. It takes effort to get to the more ecstatic point. I think you are practicing and practicing and then it all comes together. (Mary)

Nothing like jamming down the slopes to create these exact circumstances. We can't help but let go into what's happening. No time for thinking about other things and drifting off in our mind. These are precisely the right conditions for being in the Zone. I particularly experience this speeding through the trees (normally considered challenging), as there's no space for anything, but totally attending to the precise moment.

This individual concurs:

It is funny, it seems to me that what really brings me more into the Zone is when my body is involved. The more I enter into the zone, the more aware I become of my body, really into my body, my center of gravity, different sensations, more primal. Everything does itself. My mind doesn't decide. It is not that my mind is completely gone, either, it's that my mind is in my body, paying attention to my life in my body. It's a constant pushing forward, challenging myself that opens this up. (John)

As discussed earlier, most people in society operate unconsciously in pursuit of goals they've been programmed to believe they want. Our Conditioned Self runs our life mostly without our conscious awareness. As such, learning to ride the slopes becomes more difficult because we're out of tune with our natural rhythm. Whereas letting go into attending simply to what is, and I mean very much to the specific moment and to what is happening in our body, releases our true talents and natural skiing ability in a totally effortless way. Pushing past our limits serves this purpose.

Prerequisite 3: The activity must provide the opportunity for continually challenging ourselves to breakthrough to new levels of performance.

This third prerequisite to creating paradigm shifts is continually challenging ourselves to new heights of mastery. This means we don't push the limits just once, but need room for ongoing growth. Skiing is perfect for that as the room for skill progression is almost limitless. After all, there are always plenty of opportunities at our favorite ski resort for being a little on the edge (maybe literally).

One rider describes it this way:

You need to push the envelope, challenge yourself, live on the edge of losing it versus entering the zone. It needs to be something that you push further than you just did. Yes, when I purposely put myself in the position to see if I can get out of it, then it begins to happen. If I am doing the same thing that I've already done, then I can't get into the zone at all. It happens without conscious thought. Let the thoughts and actions become one so that there is no space between the two. If there is space between the two, you are too late if you are in any kind of a critical situation. When there is space between the two, you are out of the game. (Brad)

Pushing the limits allows us to regain conscious control of our ability to focus attention and break free from automatization. It makes sense then that we need room to continue to push through our current limitations. As a result, we're able to break through and mobilize our innate talents on an ongoing basis. A number of studies have demonstrated this connection between the embodied total attention experience, suspension of thought processes, and peak performance. (Abelson; Alexander et al.; Bandura; Csikszentmihalyi; Hamilton et al.; Langer; Langer & Imber; Langer & Piper; Maslow; Pratto; Strube et al.; Taylor & Fiske) This was confirmed in my dissertation as well. Pushing the limits of our abilities naturally results in ongoing experiences of the Zone.

Rarely do we get this type of opportunity in life to involve ourselves with something that liberates us from our conditioned habits and perceptual filters. Fortunately, skiing is one such sport that beckons us to discover our limits, both physically and psychologically. So, what could stop us then?

Fear

Nothing restricts fun or letting go like fear! Any skier is intimately familiar with fear and how difficult it is to just let go and groove when fear is present. Of course, nothing restricts feeling fully alive and vital in life like fear either. Fear causes us to constrict, get in our heads and disconnect from the joy in the moment.

Anytime survival is in question, of course, fear is going to arise. So put a person in somewhat foreign conditions (foreign to everyday life) on equipment that is awkward, like long skis, and it's the perfect set up for fear to occur. This can ruin anyone's day (or vacation). Just facing what seems like a steep slope can instantly trigger fear.

Certainly, skiing is a ripe feeding ground for fears to get stirred. There is the fear of falling, fear of losing control, fear of looking stupid, fear of not being good enough, fear of disapproval and let's not forget, fear of death! Similar fears may be experienced if new to skiboards as well.

Physiologically speaking, fear serves a vital function. It warns us of impending danger. Fear tells us that to feel safe and comfortable again, we simply need to avoid the situation, to flee or resist, if possible. As a result, fear and anxiety usually diminish. If we're facing a life-threatening situation, we certainly want this fear reaction to kick in, of course.

However, what if we're just imagining a negative outcome of a situation, thinking that it would be terrible if it happened? Physiologically speaking, fear still kicks in just like usual, as our system can't distinguish between real or imagined threats. Even imagining a potential danger, we'll begin to experience resistant and anxious behaviors. Now, though, it's just in our imagination and doesn't really benefit us.

For example, one such fear-based reaction on the slopes is the tendency to pull back away from the downhill slope. This makes sense logically to pull away from the slope and dig in our heels. Old fear patterns of going too fast and losing control trigger an often unconscious response. Of course, when gravity is pulling us down a slippery slope, putting our weight back to the heels is not the right reaction. What happens? We go faster, most likely the opposite of what we really wanted, and not being over our edges, we can lose control. I'm sure we've all had a taste of this before.

Breaking down the experience of fear, notice that there are three basic components: 1) A perceived sense of danger; 2) The feeling of being vulnerable, and; 3) The belief that we're unable to handle it. The perceived sense of danger, while seeming very real, is often due to our imagination, as is feeling vulnerable as a result. Then there is the 'belief' that we may not be able to handle it. We know where we got that one! Most fear reactions can be traced to past conditioning. Memories, old habits, unconscious beliefs and a culture of fear continually feed this tendency.

It's important to realize that whenever we want to progress, to succeed, to achieve new results, to learn something unfamiliar in life, we can count on fear being present. The classic approach-avoidance conflict sets in and we may find ourselves at a stalemate. While we want to move forward, the voice of fear says, 'Wait, hold back, there is possible danger here.'

However, playing it safe is not where the fun is. Yet, early cultural training encourages caution at the expense of curiosity, safety at the expense of adventure. This is where pushing the limits becomes essential if we want to ignite an awakening and break through this conditioning. To be fully functioning, a resistance to enculturation (paradigm paralysis) is mandatory. This means riding slightly more at the edge of our abilities to insure that an element of fear (or concern) can be stirred! Not too much, but just enough for us to pay attention.

The restrictive worldview we've all been exposed to hides just behind these very fears. As one researcher remarks, "Any real change implies the break up of the world as one has always known it, the loss of all that gave one identity, the end of safety." (Baldwin) Fear tells us to back off so we can feel safe again. Yet, facing our fear is the domain of break through, of paradigm shifts, of true liberation. Kind of a dilemma!

So, how do we know when fear is operating and holding us back from realizing more of our potential? Are you human? Then it most likely is! Our culture is dominated by fear. Assuming we recognize that fear is present, it then comes down to whether we want to move forward or stay stuck. To allow fear to influence our decision means continuing to be caught in avoidance and therefore driven by unconscious patterns. Attention will not focus, but remain imprisoned by past conditioning and negative drift. This is not how we progress.

Within the experience of fear lies the answer. Stepping into our fears, "Marks the rebellious dissatisfaction with life in bondage and hence provides the motive to heed the call to authenticity." (Shoham) When we choose to face our fears, we must then rise to the challenge. Now fully present, our natural instincts can awaken. Living life on the edge, we're able to step outside the influence of consensus trance, even if briefly, and this is where the real joy is. This is where we leave behind the hum drum and mediocre life also. That which stirs fear can set us free.

If we desire to create paradigm shifts in our skiing and life, to break free from paradigm paralysis, what is required is a change of orientation regarding fear. As Marilyn Ferguson states, "Anything that disrupts the old order of your lives has the potential for triggering a transformation." Yes, this will most likely prove uncomfortable, as all paradigm shifts often are at first, but there is so much to gain.

Transforming Fear

What if fear really stops us in our tracks though (literally)? For many skiers, dealing with fear is more difficult than learning to ski. If we're pushing the limits, we're going to get familiar with our fears. Here is a mindful process to use when fear arises that will enable you to remain in focused attention and stay present (rather than in resistant behavior).

The first step is noticing when fear is present. Fear may not always be easy to recognize, however. It can show up as a physical symptom rather than an emotion, such as sweaty palms, shortness of breath or tightness in the stomach. It can also show up as a mental symptom, such as doubt, worry, confusion, discouragement, disinterest and other typical avoidance behaviors. It's quite possible to not recognize fear is present as a result of being accustomed to these (now unconscious) disguises.

Recognize that fear is present and take a moment to feel it.

Yes, allow fear to be present. Feel it, recognize it and be with it. If symptoms (disguises) arise instead, trace it back to the feeling of fear. That's right, attune to it, focus attention on it, feel it. This process by the way works not only on the slopes, but in life as well.

As fear is recognized, stop, tune in and locate where fear is located within the body. This is important. Getting out of intellectualization and being in touch with the actual physical sensation keeps us present to what is. By the way, this process of working with fear also trains the attention, which is critical to learning to ski instantly.

Be with this fear reaction for a few moments. Take time to notice where fear exists within the body. It could possibly move to different areas, so allow the attention to gently follow it. Feel it, without any judgment or analysis. As it starts to fade, which may take a moment or a few minutes, it's then time to move forward again remembering to continue to stay present, whether it's taking a deep breath or pushing off down the slopes again.

Don't discount this approach as too simplistic. This is a powerful skill to develop. Normally, when fear shows up, what happens is a habit of analysis, avoidance and resistance (all mental, all left brain). This is not transformative. Feeling it, or recognizing the disguises of fear to know fear is present, and then feeling it, allows a transformation in our relationship to fear, as well as enabling us to regain the focus of our attention. This is a bypass.

Facing fear is the direct path to breaking the grip of the Conditioned Self that keeps us stuck in consensus trance. Fear points the way to what excites us (fear and excitement being identical chemically in the body). In my own years of working with thousands of private clients, I know this truth about fear, FEAR IS A VERY POWERFUL ALLY. Whenever we're challenging ourselves, pushing through our limitations, fear often shows up. Fear shines the light on the direction we must go if we really do desire to ignite paradigm shifts and realize our unique potential.

Attending to the moment means attending to whatever is occurring. If it's fear, attend to it. Not only are we being mindful to what is present, in the case of fear, but also we're then more able to stay present with fun as a result of this practice. Instant skiing and instant improvement follow along with this habit of staying present with what is really happening. In other words, let go fully into the experience, no matter what.

This process of simple attention to what is, in this case fear, is a powerful transformational process. Tuning into our fears breaks up the drift of unconscious habits of avoidance instilled by our cultural conditioning. Attending to fear present in the body, and allowing it to do it's thing until it fades will allow the energy tied up in fear to convert. What does it convert to? Joy! Breaking with our typical conditioned responses can liberate greater energy, clarity and passion.

Staying mindful to the present moment is referred to as the Zen approach to sports. This state of full attention or mindfulness to the moment is what can move us into the state of total freedom and joy. At the same time, the need to control, remember and manage things just fades or weakens. Inner chatter subsides.

Pushing past old limitations, old habit patterns and fears, a deeper, freer part of us emerges. As we practice letting go on the slopes, we're also learning to flow in all other areas of our lives. Skiboarding truly can become our time of tuning in, even our meditation or Zen practice, used to create all manner of breakthroughs in our life!

One skiboarder offers:

Skiboarding has dramatically increased my level of performance and hence my freedom on the slopes. All kinds of opportunities have opened up to me as my skill level took a quantum leap. I think the two go hand in hand, greater performance = greater freedom. Skiboarding to me is about freedom, connection, simplicity, and of course fun. (Alison)

While I'll explore this later, I want to mention that self-actualizing or fully functioning individuals, those who are having regular peak experiences, demonstrate this very ability to accept, even welcome fear. Why? They know that fear points the direction to continued personal liberation and transformation. Mostly, our cultural training teaches us to avoid fear, instead processing it in our heads through analysis, dissection and rationality. Yet, being present with what is, is the way out. So, like it or not, if we all are really committed to becoming all that we can be, and succeeding in life on our own terms, fear is definitely one of our best allies.

PART III

Grooving with Gravity

Imagine, just riding skiboards and transforming your life at the same time! This is what I'm talking about! Breaking through the paralysis of paradigms frees you to live to your unique potential in life. It is quite rare to find something so immediately effective that can do this.

CHAPTER 9

Body Wisdom

It's changed my whole awareness of myself as a creative person. Now it's spilled over and I find myself building a whole life around being in the Zone and being creative and living from that space. It is spreading definitely. It is contagious, the more you go into the Zone, your body gets accustomed to living out of that space. You get information about your real self through these activities, and your whole life is changed around because you based it around something real, self-actualizing, rather than something you do.
- John -

I believe that to truly experience instant skiing and instant fun, it's necessary to understand paradigm paralysis and how our tendency towards left brain domination can inhibit our chances for learning to ski instinctually. Now armed with this knowledge, it can be much simpler to notice when we're no longer present, instead captivated by old conditioned programs and fears, and therefore locked into attention drift.

Focused awareness dramatically enhances performance. Being in our head, thinking about what we should be doing, doesn't. Skiing is a physical sport as it's all about our bodies learning how to adapt and move. It's NOT about gaining intellectual mastery nor is it about trying. These cause internal division, separating us from what is happening. Subsequently, we lose contact with the direct feedback necessary to move fluidly and navigate the changing terrain and conditions.

As one rider describes her experience:

Instead, you are completely focused on the moment, completely focused on the second really. I find that it is a form of meditation really. Being in my body fully, I feel joyous. (Liz)

Children intuitively know how to do this. They learn with their bodies, with their senses, with being in the moment. Instant skiing happens exactly this way. As adults, mostly our body wisdom lies dormant, awaiting reactivation. What reignites this wisdom is recapturing the ability to focus our attention and use it to stay present, and more specifically, stay embodied.

Incorporating the prerequisites for creating paradigm shifts allows us to even more quickly regain control of our attention and focus it to the fully embodied, joyful moment. Reframing our approach to skiing based on this deeper understanding can aid not only in an accelerated learning curve, but ignite instant fun and regular peak experiences as well.

Fear in contrast creates tension and rigidity in the body. As such, it creates a tendency to get into our heads, a natural defense mechanism, adding to increased doubt and intellectualization. Fear throws us into the old habits of attention drift, disconnecting us from the focus needed to respond to the moment. I suggested a technique earlier to use fear as a way to stay present. Keeping our attention focused on what's happening right at the moment aids in keeping the conditioned mind from intervening.

This automatic and unconscious mechanism to react to fear may be difficult to redirect at first. Instead of being in the present moment, we may find ourselves trying to remember what worked before, what we were taught, how to turn or move like we did last time or how hungry we suddenly became. The moment is lost, no longer in the here-and-now, we lose our center and instead disconnect from what is attached to our feet and the ground. This is not a safe way to ride.

Different from walking on solid ground, skiing requires us to be able to glide without a firm foothold, while being pulled downhill by gravity. This is often an awkward feeling for beginners. It's a whole different set of circumstances for our bodies to adapt to. Yet, our body is naturally equipped to rebalance itself and adjust to differing angles and sensations automatically.

Now I'd like to introduce one more element. Being that the body has a wisdom of its own and will naturally acclimate when riding the slopes, I'd like to recommend allowing your attention at first to be just on the physical experience. Forget pushing the limits at first. That comes later after you no longer are learning the equipment. Like attending to fear when it's present, attending to the body is a great way to stay present and not fade off into old patterns of thought and behavior.

Focus your attention simply on what's happening in your body very specifically. This means fine tuning your ability to attend to all the micro-sensations and subtle movements that are occurring. I mean, really focus as you turn, lean, edge, stop and stand. This is what will disengage you from the trance of attention drift.

When you're ready to do the next run, don't try to recall what worked on your previous run. Just let go and be in full attention in your body to what is really happening on this run, right under your feet. The natural wisdom inherent in your body will know what to do instinctively. As I say this, this needs to be understood not on an intellectual level, however. Drifting into the mental conversation of 'how' will only delay this process.

One person describes it this way:

You are aware and adjusting to what you are doing, but you are not fixated on anything. It just flows. I think that one of the biggest factors is the challenge that it presents. Definitely, the challenge and being able to create the outcome has a lot to do with that. Yet when you are in it, you don't feel that you are on the edge. Feels like total calm. (Jeff)

Being in total control is really an illusion anyway. How can we possibly keep track of the immensity of essential ingredients that are required to ski correctly, such as body position, varying terrain and conditions, stance, edges, direction, feet, knees, snow conditions, weather, other people on the slope, our fear, etc. We're not really even in control of our basic bodily functions. Are we in control of our heart beating or our breathing when asleep?

So much of life is out of our conscious awareness and control anyway.

However, the Conditioned Self, trained to think it's in control, just habitually stays stuck in unconscious limitations and false beliefs. The ego-mind is not in control, but it thinks it is and believes it needs to be. So when fear presents itself, this is exactly the moment to choose to stay present, and sidestep all those ego-driven defense mechanisms that pull us out of the moment.

Discovering that our bodies know exactly what to do is a true blessing. This innate wisdom could be described as "the essential and instinctive body consciousness which can see and do what is necessary without any mental thought." (Sri Aurobindo) Skiboards automatically allow this instinctive body consciousness to guide us, allowing our unique natural rhythms to ignite, such that we can let go and groove with gravity. It's a perfect match.

I believe in the power of skiboards and our bodies knowing exactly what to do at the right moment. Many skiboarders would say, just get on skiboards and go! Within this simple wisdom lies the truth. Our body learns faster without our head (or ego) getting in the way. So here is the fast method to learn how to skiboard: *put them on, find an easy downhill slope to start with, and go!*

However, I don't feel I'd be doing my readers justice if I didn't offer a few more suggestions compiled from my many years of experience. My intention is to offer you ideas that can help to accelerate your learning curve even more. Following are typical situations and conditions you may come across when riding skiboards.

Remember the previous discussion about staying present, in the body, and letting go into the experience. Pay particular attention now to the micro-sensations within your feet, posture, the feel of your skiboards, edges and the ground. Just BE HERE NOW on skiboards gliding on the snow. Focus exactly to what's happening in your body while riding.

First Time Riding?

If this is your first time ever at the ski slopes, I suggest getting used to your skiboards at home. After adjusting your boots to your bindings, put your boots and skiboards on in your living room. Allow your stance to be natural, standing upright as you normally would, with knees slightly bent and body in a relaxed position.

Imagine for a moment just riding down a run, leaning slightly to the right and then left as you go down. We're just doing a simple visualization to start. Like a bird riding in the wind, see your movements as graceful, continuous and flowing.

Now, follow this by physically leaning, to the left, then right side of your body. Place your attention on your feet as you lean and notice the subtle movements as you roll your feet from one side to the other. Slow it down and speed it up and keep attending to the sensations. Feel the support of your boots and how they interact with your bindings and skiboards also.

Next, get a little more aggressive with your leans. Put both of your skiboards on their edges, first leaning to one side until both skiboards lift up slightly on one side and your weight goes to the inside edge of one, outside edge of the other, in unison. Then lean the other way. A wall for support may help. As you do this, attend fully to all the subtle movements in your body (head to toe). You're not only getting the feel of your equipment, but also signaling your body to connect to the feel of riding.

Continue to get used to your skiboards. Try lifting them up off the ground, one at a time, to feel the weight. Attend to the extra extension, both in the front and back of your boots, as you lift them, getting more familiar with their length. Remember, this is not a mental exercise, but instead a way to allow your body to adjust to various positions and build familiarity.

Now, try leaning forward, just slightly, and then backward a little, to find your limits front and back. Get a feel for the flex of your boards and how they bend in the middle as you put your weight in different places along the length of them. Continue exploring your skiboards, boots and the interaction with the floor.

Next, stand with boots and skiboards on a simple throw rug or scatter rug on top of a polished floor. With weight balanced and knees slightly bent (in a relaxed position), turn both feet together to the left. The rug should move as you do this. After that, turn your feet together to the right. Keep your shoulders facing straight ahead while you're doing this. Now keep it going, turn left, then turn right. Get into a rhythm. Try to do at least ten continuous turns. Let your posture be relaxed, upright and arms swinging freely.

The main idea is to slide the rug in one direction, then the other. If this isn't smooth and easy, you may be putting your weight too far forward or back or the rug is sticking. Otherwise, just stay centered, upper body pointing straight ahead while turning from your waist. You don't have to make big swings left and right. You only need to turn maybe 30 to 45 degrees each way.

Congratulations, you can now do parallel turns! Time to get on the snow!

Hit the Snow!

The second phase of tuning into your skiboards is at the resort. Get on the snow and do a simple warm up. After your boots are in your bindings of course, get used to twisting to turn. Start twisting your feet together pointed in the same direction, towards the left, then right, and let your bases glide across the snow. You'll be making just partial twists one way, then the other, just like at home.

Attend to the feeling from your feet all the way up to your upper body as you move. It's best to do this in one continuous movement. This is what you'll do when coming down the mountain as you make turns. It's just a simple twist. What you're doing is pointing your skiboards in the direction you want to go.

After you're used to this twisting motion, now try skating forward to get comfortable with this motion as you push off on one while gliding forward on the flat base of the other. Now, alternate one foot to the other like you were skating on snow. Skating makes it easier to get to the lift and is also the same motion you can use to traverse on the flats. It's an important skill to get familiar with.

Remember, this is all about attention and breaking from the old ways of intellectualization and fear. Continue to focus your attention easily, noticing what's happening in your body. Stay out of what might happen next, a long engrained mental pattern. Your body will get the feel of your skiboards and naturally know what to do.

If you're still feeling a bit reticent about going right to the lift, find a slight incline nearby, and just climb the hill sideways. Go up a ways and then point down and as you glide down, twist your skiboards together in parallel, slightly in one direction and then the other to make turns. Your body will learn as you do and know how to find its balance. Stance is upright, unlike putting your weight to the front tips as with managing long skis.

One time I was introducing skiboards to a local resort in New Mexico and training ski instructors. The first ski instructor and student went up on skiboards. Within about twenty minutes, the ski instructor came back down without the student. I asked what had happened. He said that after they got off the lift, they rode together for about fifteen feet. The student turned around to look at him, and said, "Thanks, I got it" and took off. He had no one to teach so he rode down alone, trailing his student. The student got down before him and got right back on the lift before he got down. It can really happen that fast. Not great news for ski instructors, however!

Natural Stance

Finding your natural stance will come easy. However, I would like to offer my suggestion here as just something to be aware of. The best stance for skiboarding is upright, knees relaxed that is quite similar to the stance in many martial arts or even snow-boarding. Take Tai Chi, for example. The basic standing Tai Chi meditation and stance is upright, with knees slightly bent, shoulders back and head upright. This position allows energy to flow (called chi) connecting the lower half of the body with the upper half. When chi flows, we experience more clarity, energy, and aliveness, which is exactly what is the experience for most skiboarders.

Open the chest area by bringing the shoulders back in a straighter position, but without straining. The stance needs to be relaxed, but upright. This is one reason why skiboarding can be so addictive. It causes us to get back to our natural stance, thereby allowing Chi or life force to flow. This results in an immediate experience of greater energy, joy and clarity of mind.

This is the natural stance we gravitate to when riding skiboards. However, it's possible due to poor habits of posture in life (or previous skiing) to bend forward with shoulders drooped (like a gorilla stance). This doesn't allow Chi to flow. In this position, fatigue can set in, as well as a host of other energy related health issues. Oxygen can't flow either. Find this upright stance position and it may easily begin to transfer into how you carry yourself in other arenas of your life.

The Lift

First, choose the right lift. If this is your first time, choose a lift that takes you to beginner (or green) runs. My first time on long skis ever, I got on the wrong lift (thanks to my friend) and ended up on a black (advanced) run. Big mistake, especially on 200 cm skis, on ice, at night!

I would recommend the beginner runs for everyone, no matter the skill level, just at first. Getting the feel of your skiboards and attending to your body is easiest here. As I am suggesting a shift to being attentive in the moment to the subtle physical move-ments, beginner runs are a great place to start. Even advanced riders can benefit from taking some time to focus to these micro-sensations as they play with different carves and movements.

If you're already a good skier, you can go to an intermediate groomed run at first. Remember skiers, don't 'ski' these, in other words, don't lean forward on them. Think skating, if you've ever skated. Stay upright and centered and don't lean forward over the tips or too far back either. Take a run to attend to the sensations and play with different moves however, and your skills will improve immensely.

As an aside, personally I ride many different skiboards. Even though I've been riding for many years, I find that it still takes a run or two to get used to the characteristics of a particular pair of skiboards. They all have a slightly different feel to them. So whether this is your first time, or first time on one pair of skiboards, allow yourself some time to get the feel of what is on your feet and go to a slightly easier run to start.

Lifts are probably the most intimidating experience you'll have, especially if you're a total beginner. Good news! Lifts are way easier on skiboards than long skis. Not only do you have more ability to maneuver in the lift lines, but also getting on and off the lift is a delight. Skiboards being lighter on your feet, will also allow for more enjoyment even while just sitting on the lift as they won't pull so much on your knees.

1) Getting to and on the lift:

If there's a gradual slope going to the lift, you can use the simple snowplow (pizza wedge they call it) to inch your way forward and check your speed. Angle your skiboards so the inside edges dig in a little, coming together at the tips. An alternative is to just park your boards sideways to the fall line and dig in on the edges and skid (see later).

Here is where poles can come in handy. Poles can help to check your speed so you don't run into the person in front of you. Mostly, though, you'll get used to being in the lift line and as anything else, adjust to it quite naturally, and much faster on skiboards.

One more tip. If you've never been on a lift before, you could get a 'getting on and off the lift' lesson from the ski school. You'll most likely find that it usually comes quite easy however after a try or two. Remember, everyone goes through this at first no matter what they're riding (and much more difficult for snowboarders at first). We've all had the lift operators stop the lift for us at one time or another (or maybe it was just me).

Getting up to the lift, just stop at the line or gates (where everyone else is waiting to get on). As the lift goes by, move forward to the next line (where you mount). You can just shuffle up. Wait for the lift to catch up to you from behind (make sure to look behind you) and just sit down. Keep your tips up and facing forwards so your tips don't catch on the snow. Catching on the snow may mean they pop off or worse yet, pull you off the lift chair (embarrassing as they have to stop the lift). Now, just sit back, enjoy the ride and be prepared to answer questions about skiboards from fellow lift riders.

2) Getting off the lift:

You'll see the 'Dismount' line coming up and people getting off the lift ahead of you. As you get close, put the safety bar up (if it's down) and move more to the edge of your seat. Put at least one hand on the edge of the seat so you know where it is and to prevent yourself from falling off.

Keep your tips up slightly so they don't dig into the snow as you're dismounting. As your skiboards first contact the ground, just stand up with your knees and keep your skiboards pointing forward. Push off with your hand that is remaining on the seat. Lean forward just enough to match the angle of the slope (perpendicular to the slope) and head down. Stay centered, not leaning forward too much, and not leaning to the back tails either.

You just want to ski off the chair. Don't let the chair push you. Don't forget to use at least one hand to push off the chair. You don't have to be concerned about getting away from the chair, just move forward off the chair and down.

Now skate over to the top of the run so you're facing down and ready to go. Let your skiboards start gliding forward down the hill, according to your comfort level. Gravity will do all the work. Just stand up naturally on your skiboards, with knees slightly bent. Keep your weight centered (not too far forward and not too far backwards). Let go!

For those who've already taken ski lessons, you may be relieved. No more leaning towards your front tips, using your hips or whatever else they taught you to manage those long sticks. It's really better to just forget those 'how to ski' techniques entirely and retrain yourself naturally based on your own instincts.

Let the experience be fresh and new. Treat yourself to a whole new adventure. Rather than your head leading, let your body lead. This is the time to get acquainted with the wisdom of your body.

If you're a skier and intend at some point to ride your long skis again, just follow this method of attending to the micro-sensations within your feet, legs, upper body, and tuning into the whole physical experience. Learning this approach will translate to improving your long ski riding (if you can talk yourself into going back to long skis that is).

Stopping

I've only ever been on skis for two weeks total in my life, so I didn't know how to parallel stop yet. What can I say, it took me about two seconds to pull off a perfect parallel stop! I was amazed! And, so were my friends.
(Christine)

Knowing how to stop is definitely a good idea. So, before you go too far down the slope, practice stopping. Once you get a little momentum going, here are a few options in order of preference:

1. **Hockey stop.** Keep your skiboards parallel (pointing in the same direction equally distanced apart), turn sideways against the slope (perpendicular to the downhill slope). Now use the inside edge of the lower one, the outside edge of the upper one and dig in the edges until you come to a halt. You'll need to lean uphill slightly while doing this and have some speed going for it to work.

2. **Snowplow to a stop.** Front tips angled in towards each other to form an upside down 'V' with back tips angled open and front tips almost touching. Dig in on your inside edges of both skiboards, particularly towards the centers of your edges and slow down to a stop. The more pressure on your inside edges, the more you slow down. Fortunately, with skiboards you don't have to worry so much about crossing your tips.

3. **Head uphill.** Just turn your skiboards more uphill on a carve until you slow down, just being sure you don't over rotate your shoulders and go too far uphill. Doing this would cause you to start going backwards and you don't want that just yet – or do you?

4. **Fall.** It's effective, but not as pleasant. Sometimes, though, it's the best option in a pinch.

The thing about stopping is to not get in your head. This includes over analyzing what I am suggesting to you. Let your natural instincts take over and be in the flow. Your body if you're attending to it, will naturally figure it out. Your attention needs to be on your skiboards and the ground.

Once you get the hang of stopping at slower speeds, now go a little faster and stop again. Keep doing this until you're comfortable stopping at a variety of speeds and on various terrain. Work your way up to faster and faster speeds, of course, within your comfort range. Learning to stop doesn't really take very long.

Skidding

Skidding means allowing your skiboards to glide sideways down the slope, while parallel to each other (pointing in the same direction). This offers another means of control. It will give you the ability to easily handle any uncomfortable terrain.

To skid, start by facing sideways, perpendicular to the slope, stopped, with edges dug in (uphill facing edges on both skiboards). Now, begin to release the pressure on your edges slightly so that you begin to skid or slide down the hill on your bases. Just a little relaxed pressure will do. Allow yourself to glide sideways downhill a little faster and then dig your edges in again. Try this facing the other way as well.

Skidding is valuable when you want to get down something perhaps too steep for comfort or if you're tired and want to take a break, but still keep moving. It's a good skill to be familiar with. Notice the control that you have with this technique.

As with all my suggestions, put your attention fully on what's happening. Put your attention in this case on your edges and bases, your feet and the pressure on the sides of your ski boots. Notice this movement of sliding sideways on the snow on your bases and notice when you dig in with your edges to stop. Once you get skidding, you have another means of handling the slopes, no matter what you find yourself on.

Carving

One of the most important abilities in skiing is learning to carve turns. Carving provides you not only with great control, but also the opportunity to flow easily into peak experiences as your rhythm emerges. Carving parallel turns is in essence creating the letter 'S' in the snow behind you. Parallel turns accelerate your learning curve dramatically. With this ability, you can control your speed at will, by either aiming slightly more downhill or moving farther sideways.

Traditionally, ski schools teach the snowplow ('V' position or pizza slice) as a way to begin riding and still have some control. Yet, at some point, students then need to unlearn this technique to be able to make parallel turns (the true goal in skiing). Being easier to balance and turn on, skiboards create instant comfort. As a result, you don't need to use the snowplow (unless it's fun for you).

To carve parallel turns on skiboards requires only standing naturally and comfortably. Stay centered over your skiboards, with equal weight between the fronts and backs of your feet. Always, remember to attend fully to the physical sensations within your body. It helps to start out with an easy groomed run for this purpose.

As you begin downhill, choose a spot to turn. Now, simply twist your feet together with them pointing in the same direction, perhaps at a 30 degree or 45 degree angle, either towards the left or right across the slope. It's an easy twisting motion. You've already practiced this on the floor or flat ground in your warm up exercises.

As you twist or carve your turns, one way and then the other, notice that your downhill skiboard, no matter what direction, always has a little more weight on it than the uphill. The inside edge of the downhill skiboard is now cutting a groove in the snow. If it's not, then angle it until you feel the edge is digging in a little more. At the same time, your uphill ski is just following along in parallel. Attend to the weighting in your feet, knees and where the pressure points are in your boots.

Notice also that the more you put your weight on the downhill ski, and specifically the inside edge, the more you carve (and grip). Your ankles and knees (especially the downhill leg) are both pushing slightly towards the ground. It's a fluid motion, so allow yourself to let go into the experience, while finding your natural rhythm.

If you're attending to what is happening when you're carving parallel or 'S' turns down the mountain, you're putting your weight on your downhill inside edge and the uphill skiboard is riding along or perhaps riding along with a slight pressure on the uphill edge. As you're ready to turn the other way, relax your weight off the edges, leaning slightly more downhill and twist towards heading straight downhill briefly. Then continue the twist in the other direction (leaning uphill again). Your feet are now pointing in the other direction. Your weight is now shifting to the other edges in the new direction and you've formed an 'S.'

During the moments when you're changing direction and heading down the mountain, you may feel somewhat alarmed at first (perhaps from horrible moments on long skis). Moving from one direction to the other, at some point you'll be pointing straight downhill and as you do, you'll pick up a little speed. However, as you complete the twist to the other direction, you'll be slowing down again as you move sideways across the slope. As you form the 'S' in the snow, you'll now be linking your turns.

With practice, you'll soon be experiencing a graceful flow from one turn to the other. Notice that specifically in making your turns, you're rolling your foot from going in one direction to the other. Make it more methodical and you have your linked, parallel turns, forming a true 'S' shape.

Now if carving, especially the part when you turn downhill briefly, is truly scary, then I suggest making 'Z' turns. Though less graceful, these cause a faster change in direction. This means twisting one direction, then twist the other way without rolling your feet, creating almost a 'Z' pattern in the snow behind you rather than the gradual rolling into the next turn (as with 'S' turns). Hey, it's your time to enjoy so do whatever lets you have fun. If fear still arises, then be with it, using the technique discussed earlier.

The more perpendicular you are to the slope, the slower you go, as you're going more sideways to the force of gravity. You can even angle uphill slightly to slow down even more. The more you're angled down the mountain in line with the slope when carving, the faster you go, thanks to gravity again. Long, lazy 'S' or parallel turns will do just fine to get you down anything on the mountain. Again, remember it's your time to enjoy your day, it's not a race to the finish line.

Practice (or I mean play) alternating between making larger 'S' turns, and then, making faster, tighter, shorter 'S' turns. As you do these tighter turns, you'll be using the inside edge of your downhill skiboard to dig in more. This digging in of your edges will occur naturally as you make these tighter turns and check your speed. Just feel and attend to your natural flow as you turn one way, then the other way, and notice your posture and how you're leaning.

Play a little with your edges. Try carving while you slightly lean forward and then back of the center point of your feet. Attend to the sensations in your body when turning and edging. You're just exploring what's most comfortable and seems to have the best edging power for you. Remember that different skiboards may have a slightly different sweet spot.

One customer comments:

I had skied in my younger days, when my knees were in better shape. I saw an article in the paper about five or six years ago about skiboarding and decided to try it. I rented some at a local hill and was amazed at how easy it was to get back to the same level I was on skis after all those years and how much easier on the knees they were.

Those small boards were perfect for learning how to do a skiboard carve. Each new pair I buy, increases my enjoyment of skiboarding and helps me to elevate my skill level. I love the rapid progression you can make with skiboards and how fun they are on all parts of the mountain. I like the skiboard carve feel better than skis. (Jeff)

As you practice these turns, you'll be bypassing many, many ski lessons. Not only going into parallel turns, but even more, you'll be able to easily get into more aggressive parallel turns as well. It's common for people to get parallel turns mastered before lunch and aggressive turns before the end of their first day. It is simple unschooling.

One very important general tip that is useful in long ski skiing also is to keep your shoulders facing square down the mountain continually. You'll be making your turns from the waist down, allowing your hips to rotate as you turn left and right while shoulders are still facing straight down the slope. This gives you much more control, grace and visibility for what is coming up. You can practice this at home also. This is a refined ability that will prevent over-rotating and thus the chance of possibly falling backwards. Putting your hands in front of you, or lightly on your knees, will help you to get this position quickly. Twist your turns from the waist, not shoulders.

Hands on knees will also cause you to get a little lower and this will prepare you for riding moguls, lay-it-over carves and the glades. This is an advanced riding style that will make a huge difference in your fluidity no matter what the terrain you're tackling. Not that you need to ride with your hands on your knees, but just try it until you get the feel of it. Remember to still be upright rather than leaning forward and bending.

With wider skiboards, keep them a shoulder width apart, rather than directly next to each other. Keeping them together will scrape up the skiboards and put nicks and chips in the sides as they hit each other. If you would rather have your boots and skiboards together as you ride, then consider getting the narrower width skiboards instead.

Lay-it-over Carves

These lay-it-over carves are very much unique to skiboarders. This carve is somewhere between a normal parallel ski turn and a snowboard carve. These particular carves require being familiar with riding on and trusting your edges. With higher performance skiboards (like Summit Skiboards), the more aggressive edge or side bevel (88 or 89 degrees) allows this possibility. Your skiboard edges will dig in and grip as your body is riding closer to the ground than ever before. Being able to trust your boards and how they edge allows you to let go into these turns allowing gravity to take over.

These are truly exhilarating carves. They make the groomed runs come alive with excitement. Lay-it-over carves are about all -out-speed. There's no drifting, sliding, skidding, slowing down or holding back. It's truly breathtaking being so low to the ground and feeling the increased speed that is heightened even more by the lower posture. Of course, these carves are best done without poles, as poles can definitely trip you up. This is the time to push the limits!

Lay over carves are like riding a motorcycle around a tight corner, laying the bike down into the turn. You're close to the ground with your foot pedal almost touching. You can see this in motorcycle races. If you get a chance to watch these, notice the natural rhythm they make from one turn to the other, and how easily they lay over their bikes.

As you're laying it over, your downhill leg is almost all stretched out down the mountain. Your uphill leg is bent while your uphill thigh is practically dragging on the ground (as well as your hip). In these carves, you should be able to have either one or both palms gliding along the ground. I've worn through quite a few pairs of gloves doing this!

The downhill inside edge of your skiboards is doing most of the gripping on the snow as it's angled into the ground. This is where precision skiboards are important, as the design is just made for these types of aggressive turns. One thing you may also notice is that you're naturally riding on both edges (downhill and uphill) of your skiboards.

Perhaps you may think that going so fast may get you really hurt if you slip. However, you're so close to the ground that if you lose your edge, often you just slide onto your hip and end up sitting. So in other words, though your head says to hold back, this is one of those times to allow your bodily instincts to take over, push the limits and go for it.

Linking turns in these carves, since you're low to the ground, you don't come up all the way into the upright position. Stay low. The feeling is more like a spring off of the one uphill edge briefly and then falling into the force of gravity. Then you swing it around into the other turn. Part of the thrill, besides the sheer speed, is the feeling of free fall in the transitions. There's no slowing down between turns. Just swing your hips to the other side and link your turn. Stay low.

The more you're comfortable leaning over, and getting your skiboards on their edges, the more you can handle faster speeds. Practice getting lower to the ground, knees bent and leaning more uphill. As you practice this, you'll naturally be able to carve at faster speeds. Make sure to go on at least intermediate slopes for this, as beginner slopes don't allow you to get enough speed.

Remember: Mistakes good! Fear of making mistakes is bad!

The human physiology and psychology learns from mistakes. Of course, cultural programming may have taught us otherwise, meaning mistakes are bad. The truth is our bodies learn much more quickly from mistakes. What is really the case, in life, as on the slopes, is that only fear of making mistakes will hold us back from success. Otherwise, success is our natural birthright, and it can come easily.

Finding Our Rhythm

In the unfolding of our natural rhythm, it feels more like we're just along for the ride. This is an amazing feeling because it ignites a complete let go. Leaning in a relaxed way, riding the edges, awakens a whole new dimension of joy and effortlessness. In contrast, trying to turn our skiboards or master them or remember what we should be doing kills the moment. Riding the edges, being one with the force of gravity, just like a bird, makes for an effortless flow, and mucho peak experiences.

Allowing our natural rhythm to emerge is truly breath taking. What a beautiful and graceful feeling. Relaxing into these natural 'S' turns, flowing from one turn to the next, we get to feel a depth of aliveness and exhilaration stirred from within. Simply leaning effortlessly and allowing the edges to do the work, the real feel of flowing with gravity becomes possible. This is where the instant fun really ignites. Muscles are not so much involved anymore.

One person's description captures the essence of this:

The actions are happening as though you just completely let go of everything and let something do it for you. You got to forget about yourself, which means forgetting about being afraid. Let it go. It is probably the one thing that has attracted me is that you could just let go and be yourself. Those times when you are totally yourself and totally not trying to be anything. I would call it cosmic consciousness and I'm totally tuned in. (Brad)

Want to Improve Even Faster?

Learning the particular equipment is the key. It's important that we tune into the new equipment at first. Noticing how our upper body, lower body and feet interact with our skiboards, where the edges take hold, how they respond to different forms of pressure all allow greater familiarity. In play, this comes easily, without thinking about it.

Improvement happens quickly also when playing with different ways of riding and being creative. We can try all sorts of different things. Forget about creating bad habits. That's just ski speak that really means pay for more lessons to learn to ski correctly.

Another focus is to try putting all of our weight on the downhill skiboard, lifting the uphill skiboard completely off the ground. Now we're riding on one foot. This leads to riding on and carving on one foot in both directions. Getting used to riding on one foot means becoming more familiar with using both edges of the one skiboard. To carve the other way, you'll be using the inside edge and then turning to the outside edge of the same skiboard in the other direction.

Riding on one foot opens up even more possibilities. This dramatically improves our overall skills and balance as well. Up for riding through the moguls backwards on one foot? Send us a video. It's certainly possible.

The only other tip I have for learning more quickly is to go more often. I know this is obvious, but just had to say it. "Dear, it's my meditation time. I need to go to the mountain!" or, "I have to test these new products!" (my personal favorite), or "I have to break in my new skiboards and boots!" You've got the idea?

Ah, like you can stop yourself once the thrill grabs you. It's true that the more we go, the more dramatic the acceleration of our skills becomes and the more fun we have. It's miraculous.

Riding the Back Tails

Want to make faster turns and tackle advanced terrain? Riding the back tails provides a huge forward leap in your ski abilities. This is something more readily done on skiboards though, rather than long skis.

Riding the back tails means carving off the back side-edges, rather than the middle side-edges. Notice that it's still a rolling movement, rolling the heels from one side to the other when carving, yet with most of your weight to the tails of the skiboards. The calves are usually pressed slightly against the backs of the boots. This technique allows for much quicker turns. These faster turns come in handy especially in the moguls and glades. This by the way is already a familiar feeling to those who are water skiers.

In deeper powder, riding the back tails is essential. While skiboards are great in powder, the weight needs to shift more to the tails. The front tips will naturally rise up a little. With powder, big turns aren't necessary, just slight turns while heading almost straight down the slope. The deep powder slows you down. The feel is more like floating down the mountain.

To progress in this riding style, I suggest getting higher performance skiboards that are made for supporting weight on the back tails. These are usually wider boards, with higher end construction, such as quality hardwood cores that will support greater weight to the back tails.

Skating on the Snow!

Spinning down the mountain, one foot turns, backwards through the moguls, jamming through the trees, just name it. Whatever is possible on skates, can cross over to skiboards. Truly on skiboards, skaters rule the slopes. The translation from skating to skiboards is amazing. Most skaters get the feel within one run or less!

Maurice, a skater from Montreal, Quebec offers his testimonial:

My first time on skiboards. I had just put them on and I already looked like my 200th time on skis. I was afraid at first of not having poles in my hands, but, hey, when you're skating, you don't rely on poles! From my experience, the feeling of riding skiboards is a mix between ice skates and inline skates. Cool!

For those who haven't ridden skiboards yet and if the ski resorts are still not open, treat yourself by going ice-skating, roller or inline skating. This is a great way to warm up for the season, as well as refining proper balance and turning skills. Then when it's time to hit the slopes, your muscles will be accustomed and already you'll have a greater ability to balance and turn. Trust me, once on skiboards, you'll want to ride all day, so get in shape before the season starts.

360 spins! There's nothing more alien to most skiers than skiing backwards or turning 360s (on the ground) one after another, but on skiboards they're easy. In this case, don't focus the attention on twisting your feet, but turning with your shoulders. Keep your bases flat against the slope throughout the turn. As your shoulders lead the turn, your body follows. You can break out of the 360 turn by simply bringing it around to heading back

down the slopes. Make sure your shoulders stay parallel through the turn, evenly balanced. Dropping a shoulder will usually cause an edge to dig in.

To ride backwards for a while, or fakie, just look over one shoulder, lean to your edges and carve as usual. This takes some practice, but is quite easy on skiboards (especially twin tips). You can combine this with spins or even one foot backwards carving. The possibilities are just up to your creative inspirations.

Another variation is to carve a circle uphill. You need some speed to do this. Jamming down the mountain, go into a carve but keep it going up the slope. Then like making a circle in the snow come back out the other way heading down. It's a simple roll out the other way to compete the circle. You can even do this on one foot with a little practice. This is great fun.

Remember that it's riding the edge of your limits that keeps the thrill alive and allows for the paradigm shifts. While you can have a great time in the mountains riding, pushing the limits continually breaks you out of attention drift and consensus trance. This is why I discussed paradigms previously and what awaits with a little attention on widening your circle of comfort.

Breathing

The breath is the portal. There is a surrender, a letting go in this. Essentially it is to stop your thinking and be in the moment. If you're not following your breath, then you're thinking and this fractures the awakening.
- Tom -

Not only during your beginning days, but always, don't forget to breathe. Yes, this is an advanced riding skill. Remember it's about being in the moment, breathing in life and the whole experience. Enjoy yourself. Breathing allows us to relax and become one with the experience. It puts us directly into our body (where we need to be) and takes us out of our heads. It gets us present. The breath creates the bypass necessary to circumvent drifting into conditioned thought patterns and fear. When you notice drifting or thinking, stop and breathe.

As discussed, the Flow occurs when everything is in harmony. There's a rhythm with skiing as we carve from one turn to the other effortlessly. When we're riding the edges, and letting our skiboards do the work, moments of deep peace, awe and exhilaration emerge. We truly become one with the mountain. This is Flow or a peak experience. This is what it's all about. So, also breathe this in when it's happening!

Remember, the thrill of skiboarding is experienced in the body. Breathing brings us back into the body and allows us to let go, entering into the ecstatic moment again.

A Word about Teaching Children

Remember the unschooling article? With children, just get them on skiboards or at least shorter skis than what they 'should' be riding (like a 70 cm, 80 cm or 90 cm). Tell them to go have fun! Seriously. Kids learn so much faster than adults. They're more in their bodies and their natural instincts to learn can kick in. Just start out on an easy slope and lift.

If you prefer though, you can have them go briefly through the same process of getting used to their boots and skiboards on their feet first, either at home or flat area at the resort. Another good idea is to take them to the nearest skating rink. No kidding! I did this with my kids, and they learned how to balance and turn in one afternoon. When they hit the slopes, they just took off and I had to book it to catch up.

If your kids are a little wobbly, younger or just don't listen, like mine were early on, use a leash or kid's ski harness to check their speed so they don't take off down the slopes. Ski harnesses allow your child to maintain their own stance and balance. They can then turn on their own, while giving you room to ride behind them. The harness just makes sure they don't get out of control. Teaching them lift skills of course is essential, but usually those running the lifts will slow it down for them.

DO NOT fire all these tips or suggestions at them. Kids learn naturally if you let them just play. So let them play. They'll get it quick enough and soon be waiting for you to catch up. I know!

Most important of all, don't forget to play with them!

CHAPTER 10

Terrain and Conditions

I suspect you've hit the slopes by now and have a good grasp of varying conditions and terrain. Once up and running on skiboards, handling different challenges comes quite easily, especially if you stay in your body and out of your head. True adventure is about flowing with the moment and taking it as it comes, just like a bird floating on the wind currents.

However, I feel compelled to at least offer some skiboarding tips regarding differing terrain and conditions in the mountains. Again, take these as suggestions as things to just notice, not as rules. Since you're unique, you'll find your own *unschooling* path.

The challenge of varying conditions and terrain is no different for skiboarders than it is for skiers and snowboarders. It's simply that skiboards usually make handling what comes much easier. However, there are a few differences that I'll point out.

Following are the typical challenges you may come across on the mountain, with tips on how to handle them riding skiboards. Mostly, as you know by now, you'll intuit how to respond as naturally as riding the groomed runs on a perfect day.

I. Terrain

Groomed Runs

Generally, groomed runs are – well, groomed. They're flat, relatively smooth and usually exist mostly on beginner or intermediate runs. Occasionally, an advanced groomed run may appear which is a treat. Sometimes, you get the rare opportunity to catch untracked powder on groomed runs, which is also truly amazing.

Speaking of groomed runs, now here's a real playground. This is the perfect place to make those parallel turns. However, you can also spin down the mountain doing 360s. A little steeper and you can do those lay-it-over carves. Groomed runs are great for couple's dancing, axel jumps, gracefully riding on one foot or one foot turns or riding backwards. Skiboards will stimulate your creative talents as you let go fully into the experience and just groove.

Groomed runs are a great place to enjoy the scenery and feel the pure thrill of effortlessness and floating down the mountain no matter what you're doing. However, it's a place also to practice another technique that will build your skills for the moguls and glades – carving off the back tails. There are times when you want to carve regularly, centered, but this back tail technique allows greater speed, faster carving and a higher degree of maneuverability. As mentioned, with the ability to make faster turns, you'll have no problems in the glades and mogul runs.

Moguls

I have lost count of the times I have got down a mogul run or bit of powder with more ease, style and speed than my skiing chums and been told something like 'very good, but those little skis are easier'. When I answer with 'yes they are, so why are you making life difficult for yourself?' I normally get nothing more than a blank look.
- Dave -

Whether you like moguls or not, sometimes they're inevitable, even if it's just because of a chopped up powder day. Know that moguls are way easier and much more fun on skiboards. No skis can match the maneuverability of skiboards. Moguls seem like they were made just for skiboards. It's also a great place to push past your limits.

With moguls, you get to ride up the sides of the bumps, between them or even over the tops, but with much more control. My suggestion is just let go and play in the moguls. These bump runs also fine-tune your carving skills as you can practice turning in specific places in the mogul fields, using even more precision than on the groomed runs.

Bumps definitely demand attention. With moguls, you want to perceive not just what you feel underfoot, but what is coming towards you, keeping your gaze to include perhaps one or two moguls ahead. This allows you to flow easier and move in the way you want, while at the same time, seeing what's coming next. It is another way to push the limits.

Seldom discovered on longer equipment is that moguls offer many opportunities for play. Riding over the mogul tops and discovering powder stashes just behind them is fun. Since most skiers ride the grooves between moguls, these tend to get scraped off first. Another advantage of riding up directly to the tops of the moguls is that it naturally slows you down when approaching the top. Then starting your decline, you can take an angle and carve down the backside, just as you would be turning on a groomed run. You can even get a little air off the tops, another fun variation.

Of course, if you're feeling superhuman, you can do as the professional mogul skiers do, pick a straight line and take what comes to you. For this, you need to use your knees to absorb the blows. I would not recommend this at first, as this takes some practice, but of course skiboards will make this easier as well. Get your insurance paid up.

The best skill for moguls is to be able to turn quick, as mentioned previously. If you have practiced riding off the back tails, try it in the moguls just by quickly rolling your heels from one side to the other. Carving off the back edges of your skiboards gives much more control and speed in turning.

Another suggestion for the moguls is experiment with staying lower to the ground. Get yourself low enough to touch the tops of the moguls as you go by. This gets you into the proper position to really jam. It also lets you enjoy the speed and thrilling feeling of being more at one with the terrain.

Moguls are a great training ground for glade runs. Bumps require focused attention and very much being in the moment. These are the perfect place then for breaking free and entering the land of peak experiences.

Glades

The glades are a truly magical place. I remember my first experience in the glades. At first, I was hesitant being they were marked 'Double Black'! However, it was more the psyche of it really. I went in anyway and quickly found that riding skiboards in the glades was beyond anything I had ever experienced in my life before. It was pure thrill and a rush beyond words. There is nothing that compares.

I had to stop periodically, simply due to the sheer exhilaration and joy of it. I had to catch my breath! Talk about attending in the moment. No chance here to drift off into your thoughts. All conditioning and old habits drop away fast, while you quickly become one with pure experiencing.

Glades I feel, like moguls, are just made for skiboards. Glades are like moguls in that you have to make turns in specific places. However, in place of the top of the bumps, you find trees. Intimidating at first with all the 'Warning - Expert Only' signs and trees that don't budge. Soon, though, a flow develops. The sheer joy of cruising past trees, in such a peaceful, pristine playground, is indescribable.

If you can make fast turns (especially if you're familiar with turning off the back tails), getting around the trees is no big deal. This is one of the best advantages of skiboards. Rarely can a skier or snowboarder go where a skiboarder can go in the trees, or even keep up with them. Most will just not follow you in, right from the beginning.

With tight turns, being in the moment, thinking in split seconds, speeding through the forest, I have to say this is a natural high like no other. Take your time until you build your confidence or just flirt in and out along the edges. As with anywhere else on the mountain, skiboards provide an extremely fast learning curve. I always recommend helmets anywhere on the mountain, but especially in the trees, in case you catch a low-lying branch you didn't notice that is sticking out around the corner.

There is a thrill of cruising through the trees that is hard to explain. As you wiz past the trees, turning, following your own line, a whole new experience dawns. It's silent, it's still and it's usually all yours!

Flat Traverses

As most resorts have flat areas, it's good to know how to handle them. Everyone has some difficulty with flats, especially snow-boarders. Now here, the wider skiboards can come in handy as compared to the narrower ones. Width tends to produce greater speed due to more surface area (especially with a good wax job).

One thing I suggest with traverses is that if you see one coming up, accelerate, sooner than later. This will carry you through a little farther. To accelerate, put your weight slightly to your back tails and find the 'sweet spot' (where your speed increases). Don't use your edges, just the bases.

If you find yourself stuck on a flat, and it happens to everyone, then learning to skate will make it much simpler. To skate, ride one skiboard flat, while pushing off on the other (using the edge to dig in and push off from behind). Alternating one foot, then the other, you're skating. A little practice makes perfect and it'll come easier once you gain the initial feel. This is not much different than skating on ice skates, inline skates or roller skates, except you're on a wider platform.

If you choose to use poles, then this is the time to use them. Poles just require more upper body effort. This really needs no further explanation. Use them to push you forward. Some customers buy telescopic poles just for this, otherwise they keep them in their backpacks.

Sometimes beginner runs are so flat that they can be as

challenging. That is why those riding skiboards, even for the first time, may often go right to the intermediate runs, to start out. It depends on your resort. Trust your instincts to determine your own comfort level.

One more tip: instead of finding yourself impatient to get across the flats, try thinking that this is your activity for the day, skating on snow with no particular destination in mind. A good workout is always a great thing for your body. This makes it all more relaxing. Just find your rhythm and be present with what is. Breathe it in!

Climbing Inclines

Well, climbing uphill is all kinds of fun! Usually it's not by choice though, unless you're into that sort of thing. If you find yourself in this position, and most likely you will at some point, there are three methods that work best:

1. Side step. Face sideways against the slope, both feet pointed in the same direction. Use the uphill skiboard and move it uphill, maybe shoulder width stance apart from the other. The other foot stays put and is edged into the slope holding you in place. Then, edge the top one, get a firm hold and then bring the lower one up next to the top one. Now move the top one up again and so on. You'll be facing in one direction as you do this. It's really simple, except for the climbing part. Hey, it's great exercise, and good practice for the backcountry.

2. Reverse snowplow. Put the tails of your skiboards together and the front tips apart, forming a 'V' facing uphill. Then shuffle one and then the other up the hill lifting one over the other as needed depending on the length of your skiboards. Make sure your inside edges are dug in again by angling your skiboards slightly. Some people refer to this as the duck walk.

3. Detach your skiboards from your boots and climb in your boots. Sometimes this is the easiest way, depending on

the incline and depth of snow. This is also good practice for boot packing in the backcountry.

Advanced and Expert Terrain

Being the Novice that I am, I started on the Green (easy slopes).
It was fun, but I was itching to try out the tougher slopes.
Little did I know that later that night I'd be going down
the black diamond slopes, the terrain park, and the half pipe!
Let me tell you, I never ever thought I'd see myself
in a half pipe, but these skiboards make it a piece of cake!
They truly are made for FUN RIGHT FROM THE START.
- Carl -

The signs, whether being a black diamond, double black or warnings that announce Expert Only are to be heeded. However, keep in mind that these designations were created for those on long equipment and don't always apply to skiboards. With skiboards, advanced and expert terrain are so much easier. It's also a lot safer riding on skiboards, especially if equipped with release bindings.

These terrain designations do depend on where the resort is located. Almost all ski resorts like to feature beginner, inter-mediate and advanced terrain signs so skiers have some variety. However, all advanced terrain is not created equal. For example, in Colorado, double blacks on the big mountains are very steep, usually identified by the following: you stand on the edge of the run and as you look down, you see air underneath your front tips. Falling down these runs, you may have a difficult time stopping. No matter how good you are, I advise caution.

Keep in mind though that on deep powder days, these runs are a great place to play. The deeper powder slows you down, just enough to have a relaxed time. It's not the same as when riding advanced terrain on ice or hard pack. In powder, you just float down with little effort.

The skills required to ride advanced terrain are the same as anywhere else. Stay centered on your skiboards and turn and stop like usual. To check your speed on steeper slopes, make more across-the-slope zigzags or more elongated 'S' turns. This will keep you moving more slowly. The more you carve perpendicular to the slope, the slower you go.

On steep slopes, that perhaps intimidate you, you can also use the skidding method discussed in the previous chapter. Slide, stop, slide and stop. This allows you to get down almost anything, especially combined with your ability to traverse and zigzag down the slope. These are all the skills you really need to go anywhere on the mountain.

Terrain Parks

The tricks and moves from urban and aggressive inline skating, as well as freestyle and speed slalom inline skating are those that have most profoundly influenced skiboarding in half pipes and terrain parks. The urban spirit can be observed in the skiboarder who explores the alleys of various runs by grinding the edges of the cat-tracks, going fakie (backwards) slalom down a portion of an icy slope, rail-sliding over a log in the back-country and then hucking nicely over a large hit and pulling a 360, while grabbing the base of the left skiboard in the air (underneath the beginner chairlift of course)!

The same mechanics of park tricks apply to skiboards as with long skis and snowboards. However, skiboards, being shorter, act more like skates. Since you're landing on a shorter surface, you need to be positioned more accurately for balanced landings than those longer counterparts.

Using skiboards in the half pipe, initially a little courage goes a long way, but you'll adapt quickly. As with all else, your instincts can point the way. Just let your body get used to the feel of balance as you carve up the sides. Don't worry, you can recover more quickly than on long planks. One thing to keep in mind is that if you do slip or fall, it usually means only sliding down the incline into the center of the half pipe, so no big deal.

Watch any skateboarding or inline skating videos and you can see the types of tricks they do in the wooden plank 'half pipes' or skate parks. Try them in the mountain half pipe or park and be creative. For a list of various tricks you can perform on skiboards, visit Tricks Explained in the University section of Skiboards.com.

II. Conditions

Cruising Powder

Ah, those powder days! While it might seem skiboards are harder in powder, they're really easier. Pick a straight line and go on down. No need to turn as the snow will check your speed. If you have to turn, just make slight turns off the back tails. No more trying to jump up to make a turn, like on long skis. That's because you don't have to be concerned about long front tips burying under the snow. Water skiers, you're going to excel at this!

With powder, as mentioned, it's best to be familiar with riding off the back tails of your skiboards. In other words, put most of your weight to the back of your boot and on the heels of your feet. You're then carving off the back edges of your skiboards (though not much carving as edges are not needed much in powder). This makes for a real fun time in the deep. It's times like these that all is right with the world and you feel truly blessed.

Oh yeah, one more suggestion. In powder conditions, I suggest heading towards steeper terrain than usual. Again, the snow will slow you down and the steeper incline will keep your momentum going, so it equates to the perfect speed. Get off the green (beginner) runs in deep powder. You'll notice skiers and snowboarders have trouble on those runs also.

Now if it's deep and churned up, you can play with riding in other people's tracks to gain speed or cut back into the untracked to slow down. If you do this, prepare for hitting the deep untracked powder by rocking back on your tails. In the tracked parts, you can be more centered. Deep and tracked out are often some of the hardest conditions because of this backward and then centered motion. It does take a little practice.

Hard Pack and Ice

These conditions are less user friendly. I mean, it's often like riding on slippery concrete. Best advice I have is get used to using your edges. Lean your skiboards over so the edges are digging into the ice. You'll want your edges to do the work, not you. With skiboards, there is more weight per square inch of edge, so it's easier to get grip (more like ice skates).

Ice is not the easiest to ride on, no matter if you're riding long skis, snowboards or skiboards. Since skiboards feel more like ice skates however, you can let it rip and know you can stop right when you want to (though really digging in your edges is more necessary on ice). Since you're on ice, might as well have fun so this is a great place to do some 360 spins. No obstructions!

Sharpen your edges. You can either pay to have a shop do it, or better yet, buy an edging tool, like our Pocket Edger and do it yourself (see the Appendix for Maintenance tips). With a pocket edger you can even edge your skiboards while riding on the lift if needed and it fits in your pocket or backpack, so it's very handy.

Cold and/or Windy

While everyone else is huddling in the lodge, you can be having a pleasant day out of the wind. As it's dramatically easier to ride in the glades, turning and stopping when you want, you'll find it makes for a great escape from the cold and wind. Just layer up and don't forget your helmet, both for protection, but also warmth.

Once you open this door, that is, to riding in the trees, it doesn't matter how nasty it gets. You just duck in the trees and have a quiet, calm day riding. You even get a bonus – untracked powder as any snow on the groomed runs usually blows into the trees.

As mentioned, to prepare for the trees, start on the open slopes making fast turns and picking your path down the mountain. Learn to ride more off the back tails for better powder skills, as the trees often are untracked long after the regular runs are skied off.

Another thing about windy days is often the snow is blown to the sides of the runs. Most recreational skiers avoid the edges of the groomed runs. Not you though, so go right on over there, and make your fast tight turns in the soft stuff.

Springtime Conditions

Depending on the time of season, this can be awesome, almost like powder days. The term typically used is 'corn' snow because there are small 'corn' size ice crystals that feel a lot like soft powder when riding through them. In Springtime, you may want to arrive a little later after the lifts open. This allows the ice to soften as it warms up.

If it gets late in the season, and particularly warm (as in the afternoons), there can be unexpected 'sticky' spots that will stop you dead. Best advice I have is use Zardoz Notwax – a special Teflon coating you can wipe on your bases. It makes for great glide in the sticky stuff. It also works great in slush and all Spring-like conditions. Put this on top of warm or spring temperature hot wax for an even better ride.

Spring conditions require reading the terrain and putting more weight to the back tails of your skiboards. Be careful in Springtime, you can be flying down the mountain with a smile on your face and then suddenly be stopped dead in your tracks. This has thrown many a rider to the ground as they suddenly came to an unexpected stop.

III. New Horizons

There are many variations on having fun on skiboards. Adventurous skiboarders around the world seem to come up with all kinds of creative possibilities for riding skiboards. We always love hearing about them, so write us and send photos or videos!

I've heard from skiboarders who ride behind snowmobiles with a rope tow or skate across frozen lakes. Some have used dogs to pull them on skiboards; people ride down the banks of rivers (either on snow or dirt), create their own terrain parks in their back yards or even use skiboards like snowshoes (they provide good floatation). If you loosen your boot buckles, you can even cross-country ski, though AT bindings work better for this, or even better mounting your skiboards with cross country bindings.

Special mention goes to those skiboarders who ride the sand dunes in the summers (or coal banks). This does feel like snow, but with a little more friction. Make sure to use an older pair of skiboards, as most likely you'll trash your bases. Hey, who needs winter?

Many skiboarders have taken to using kites. There are kites that are specially made to pull you across the ground or even uphill. Uphill with a kite is cool because you just hold on and when you get to the top, you get to ride back down. No lift ticket! Put your kite in your backpack and off you go. Some also use kites on flat ground like on frozen lakes to ride untracked snow. This can get you to speeds of 60 miles per hour or more depending on your location. Another opportunity for pushing the limits!

So, you don't even need to live near a ski resort to skiboard in the winter or summer. Cool!

Backcountry

Backcountry skiboarding is quite popular. Going into the back-country requires a few more precautions however, but it's free! You'll want some avalanche training, the proper equipment and knowledge of the terrain you're entering. Make sure to take a buddy and let others know where you're going. Backcountry skiboarding is not crowded, is so very peaceful and a way to combine hiking with skiboarding – a great combo.

To go backcountry, there are three basic options to get uphill:

1. You can use snowshoes to climb while your skiboards are in your backpack. Just use your ski boots (usually unbuckled) in the snowshoes and switch at the top. Put your snowshoes in the pack (maybe your poles) and down you go.
2. Mount your skiboards with special AT bindings, such as the Fritschi Diamir Freeride bindings. These have a free heel lever so you can climb uphill with ski boots in the bindings. The free heel allows you to climb easily. You'll also need skins to attach to your bases, as these will allow you to glide forward, but not slide backward. At the top, you take the skins off, click down your free heel and lock it into place. Now you have skiboards with regular ski release bindings to ride down the hill with.
3. Boot pack – just walk up in your ski boots until you get to the top and then put on your skiboards and ride down. Poles can help for better balance in the deep stuff.

Ski Dancing

Instead, you are completely focused on the moment, completely focused on the second really. I do think you have to have everything going together, both relaxation and concentration. When I'm learning the steps, I don't really hit a zone, but once I have learned them and they come easily to me, then I can enter the zone. Skills really have to be in place. When you hook them together [relaxation and concentration], which we don't normally do, that is what takes you into the zone. (Liz)

Another fun variation to try with skiboards is ski dancing (also called ski ballet). It's quite amazing to watch those who're good at it. Usually people with either a dancing or skating background can perform ski dancing on snow, especially with skiboards because they're easy to maneuver.

Ski dancing can be done singly or with a partner. Similar tricks as with skating, such as one-foot turns, spins, crossovers and more can be done. You can even lift your partner up and twirl her around. You can do regular skate freestyle moves like axels, waltz jumps and more. I'm not an expert here so I can't offer much advice, except I know it will come easier with skiboards than with other, more awkward equipment.

Let the creativity flow and just have the time of your life.
Since you're no longer concerned about what others think,
you're truly free, both on the slopes and off.

Part IV

Skiboarding and Self-Actualization

It is so hard to explain because we don't have the language. Everything, the trees, rocks, sky, ocean feel alive like they're filled with consciousness. I feel completely in an ecstatic state in that moment. At one with everything, conscious and aware of everything else. There is a feeling of totality. It isn't just the physical activity kicking off endorphins.
- Arleen -

CHAPTER 11

Realizing Our True Potential

Every organism has one and only one central need in life,
to fulfill its own potentialities.
- Rollo May -

Pushing the Limits Revisited

Being physically and actively engaged in doing something that's truly enjoyable, that challenges our limits and brings us into pure, in-the-moment experiencing, while suspending mental activity, precipitates true breakthroughs. Skiing, more specifically ski-boarding, is the perfect vehicle for confronting any psycho-logical and physiological limitations, thereby opening up a new personal dimension of optimal functioning. I know this sounds strange as a topic being discussed in an instant skiing book, but it's my experience and the experience of many, many others. I would like to touch on this briefly and share what I've discovered.

Pushing past previous mental and physical limits forces us to be fully attentive to the moment. However, the Conditioned Self, operating out of habit and previous programming, can't deal with the complexities of riding on the edge. It can't process it all fast enough, so it simply shuts down, temporarily. As a result, a paradigm shift often occurs.

While the Conditioned Self needs predictability and habits to function, pushing just a little farther than our immediate comfort zone brings us directly into the unknown. Facing not knowing what will happen next, fear often arises. While a natural response based on years of conditioning, the way out is to remember that fear is our ally. Fear, from our previous discussion, indicates that we're headed in the right direction, towards our higher potential, to greater liberation. Of course, if it becomes too overshadowing, then be in the moment and use the fear process described earlier. Otherwise, go for it!

Living-on-the-edge activities, no matter how we choose to ride, stimulate transcendence of our old, inhibitive habit patterns. As a result, our neurophysiology is reformatted so it can adapt and sustain this new expanded state. (Roshi; Suzuki; Tart; Watts; Young) Breaking free of all our restraints repeatedly – emotional, physical and psychological – instills a heightened level of aware-ness and aliveness accompanied by a host of positive changes.

As attention, normally controlled and unconsciously directed by paradigms, disengages from cultural programming, a release from our usually constricted sense of self can occur. The emergence of a more encompassing worldview, a true feeling of freedom and the joyful flow that is correlated with the experience of our Authentic Self opens up. It's during these very moments when we break out of the prison of fragmented and hypnotized attention and reawaken to the "miracle of awareness." (Ferguson) Reports from all those I interviewed in my dissertation concur. Simply put, we shift into our more vital, alive, expanded, passionate and awake self.

These jolts of awakening, as I like to refer to them, occur as a result of "an intense, single-minded attention state and, paradox-ically, this experience can occur only after we have stopped processing everyday reality [the mind shuts down]." (Csikszentmihalyi) When in this fully absorbed attention state, cultural paradigms are suspended, the usual patterns of constant inner chatter subsides and our true essence or core self emerges. Jamming down the mountain, each in our own special way, is what does the trick.

Realizing who we really are, behind the facade of social con-ditioning, freed from who we've been led to believe that we are, occurs naturally when our defenses, conditioned habits and ego-image subside. Csikszentmihalyi found this to be true in his investigations of flow during extreme sports. He reports:

In flow, the self is fully functioning, but not aware of itself doing it, and it can use all the attention for the task at hand. At the most challenging levels, people actually report experiencing a transcendence of self, caused by the unusually high involvement with a system of action so much more complex than what one usually encounters in everyday life.

What he's describing is the inability of the Conditioned Self to maintain control, instead losing its grip over attention during challenging activities. While sometimes anxiety-producing at first, transformation emerges out of the rubble. Fully absorbed in the moment, attention is no longer adrift. The focus of attention expands to encompass the full complexity of the activity at hand. As such, a new, more expanded awareness results, allowing us to step out of the constrictions of the everyday business of living consciousness.

Immediately noticeable regarding peak experiences is that the learning curve dramatically accelerates. This is something I've personally witnessed with skiboards in particular, as compared to skis. Research supports this connection between rapid skill acquisition and the regular occurrence of these peak moments. (Csikszentmihalyi) It's at these times that the wisdom of our body takes over, allowing an instantaneous instinctual learning to take place. Skill acquisition is no longer hindered with distractions. Physiological adaptation to new skills is quicker now, when not inhibited by the mind. In short, peak experiences cause us to get better faster.

It's precisely in stepping past our comfort zone, pushing past our psychological and physical boundaries, that creates this transformation. Of course, I'm saying that each has their own way. It's not about the opinions of others. It's about our personal evolution and treating ourselves to instantaneous peak moments of fun our way.

Peak Experiences

Instant fun means having frequent peak experiences. I feel the faster we can spark these, the more incredible the run. Peak moments of effortless flow are almost indescribable. In flow, we're completely absorbed, one hundred percent engaged like a child involved in pure play, with our instincts leading the way. During these moments, we're no longer focused on learning or anything else. We're fully alive in the moment.

These joyful moments of absorbed attention or peak performance are often characterized as a feeling of union and merging with the total mountain experience. Accompanying this feeling of oneness is the natural dissolution of previous constrictive life patterns. (Allen; Csikszentmihalyi; Eidelberg; Grof; Hollaq; James; Laski; Maslow; Pahnke; Thomas & Cooper). These and other researchers find that this paradigm shift into total absorption while in the midst of activity, causes the usual division between experiencer and the experience to totally disappear. The result is this feeling of oneness, of unity and harmony.

In contrast to passive meditation methods, these moments of mindfulness on the slopes are like a meditation in action. While certainly, similar experiences have been attained by those practicing more passive methods of meditation, being in activity, present in the moment and fully engaged in pushing the limits of performance seems to be the more powerful path to sparking these frequent peak moments. (Dhiravamsa; Fromm; Goldstein; Goldstein & Kornfield; Kasamatsu & Hirai; Koplowitz; Kornfield & Breiter; Nyanaponika; Roberts; Thoreau)

It's not surprising that certain Zen mindfulness (active meditation) techniques as well as teachings from various martial arts, such as Aikido and Tai Chi have been used to train skiers and other athletes. (Tart) The Zen-like instruction involves suggestions such as being here now, total attention to the moment and unlearning the tendency to be judgmental and self-critical. (Herrigel; Gallwey; Nideffer; Young) I agree with these approaches as I find that being in the body, doing that which is truly joyful and moving past fears to create paradigm shifts are the direct route to instant skiing and instant life transformation.

Research provides additional supportive evidence that the body, being firmly rooted in the here-and-now, represents a direct path to transcending the Conditioned Self. Engaging in joyful physical activities, attention being totally embodied, with mental activity suspended, we break with the restrictions imposed by previous cultural conditioning. (Lowen; Marrone; Naranja; Ouspensky; Perls; Rinpoche; Rogers; Tart; Watts; Wilber) These studies, involving thousands of subjects, have clearly demonstrated that these 'embodied' total attention experiences can consistently produce ego-transcendence.

This is why I'm so passionate about the sport of skiboarding. Being so much fun and easy from the start, it naturally instills a desire to see what is possible. Pushing through our limitations usually occurs without even realizing that we're doing it. Letting go, effortlessness and joy are the immediate byproducts. We don't have to learn how to let go, we instinctively want to. Yet, there's even more happening behind the scenes as we'll soon see.

These and other defining characteristics of peak experiences are well documented by numerous researchers, spanning thousands of subjects. Peak experiences are referred to as "flow" (Csikszentmihalyi), "altered states of consciousness" (Tart), momentary experiences of "cosmic consciousness" (Bucke), "mystic or visionary states" (Pahnke; Yogananda), "blackout" (Kane), "being in the zone" (Young), and "absorbed attention states" (Quarrick), to name a few. Though having different terms, the descriptions and characteristics of these peak experiences are quite similar across all research studies. These extraordinary moments can be summarized as follows:

- A state of total concentration, fully absorbed attention
- A non-evaluating, non-comparing and non-judging cognition
- Insight into the true nature of reality, behind the illusions
- Perception is expanded, enlarged, accompanied by a greater clarity and objectivity
- The experience is ego-transcending, and self-forgetful – an experience of the real self, behind the personality facade or conditioned self
- Is intrinsically motivating, an end in itself rather than a means to an end – experiencing perfection in the moment

- Time is transcended or suspended
- There is a loss of fear, anxiety, inhibition, defense, confusion, and restraint
- An increase in spontaneity, creativity, playfulness
- Is accompanied by a deeply felt positive mood – joy, ecstasy and exaltation
- A sense of sacredness, awe, wonder, gratitude
- Experience of being here-and-now, rooted fully in the present moment
- Alleged ineffability – frequent claims that language is inadequate to describe them
- A feeling of total surrender to the experience, similar to the idea of letting go in Taoist philosophies
- An experience of unitive consciousness or a feeling of oneness with all things *(Alexander; Bucke; Csikszentmihalyi; Deikman; Eidelberg; James; Maslow; Maslow; Pahnke; Pahnke et al: Privette; Quarrick; Ravizza; Tart; Yogananda; Young)*

We've all had these times when having that special run. It all just happens effortlessly, as if it's doing itself and all is perfect with the world. During these energizing moments, we feel the pure joy of being exuberantly alive, as when we were children. This is after all what really motivates us to come back to the resort, isn't it?

Abraham Maslow, a well-respected researcher in the area of human potential, finds that having regular peak experiences can provide the ability to not only break up these old, habitual mindsets, physiologically speaking, but also awaken a deeper, more actualized part of ourselves. He asserts that the weakening of ego constraints and self-forgetfulness associated with peak experiences is "one of the paths to finding one's true identity, one's real self, one's authentic nature, one's deepest nature." Many other investigators draw similar conclusions. (James; Quarrick; Tart; Vaughan; Wilber) It's in these moments that we're performing at our best and stepping past previous boundaries into our greater potential.

One co-researcher comments:

It's changed my whole awareness of myself as a creative person. Now its spilled over and I find myself building a whole life around being in the zone and being creative and living from that space. It is spreading definitely. It is contagious, the more you go into the Zone, your body gets accustomed to living out of that space. You get information about your real self through these activities and your whole life is changed around because you based it around something real, self-actualizing, rather than something you do. (John)

In the words of another interviewee,

In normal everyday state you go through mechanistic behaviors. You are not thinking about what you are doing, you almost feel robotic. Doing rituals all day long. You aren't aware of what you are doing, or how you are doing it or what the universe around you is doing. In the zone, you all of a sudden become aware. (Arleen)

In researching difficult sports, such as mountain climbing or skiing, one investigator found that peak experiences were "almost like an egoless thing in a way – somehow the right thing is done without thinking about it or doing anything at all. It just happens and yet you're more concentrated." (Csikszentmihalyi) This is a great description of peak experiences and what in particular makes skiing so much fun. This researcher called it waking up to the "autotelic self" or Authentic Self (as I like to call it).

At these times, there's "a unified flowing from one moment to the next, in which there is little distinction between self and environment, between stimulus and response or between past, present and future." (Csikszentmihalyi) Everything melts into one joyful moment-to-moment harmonious flow. This is the feeling of oneness. No longer divided within, we feel fully alive. This is the expanded state of optimal human functioning.

Here is how another rider describes it:

You are one with world, self or God. Pure connection. It's a real high, a joyous moment. Everything feels perfect, emotionally, spiritually, physically. You get this sheer grateful attack! (Robin)

Another co-researcher shares their experience:

Things that come to mind are timelessness, freedom, alive, well-being, expanded. It seems like when I'm really fully in the zone, I have this overall internal conversation which is this big 'Yes', everything is a 'Yes'. There is no conflict. The zone to me is being or essence. An actualized sense of self. (John)

In short, paradigm shifting is all about being more capable of engaging our lives fully and living to our true potential. This is the case not only on the slopes, but pushing through our limitations in daily life as well. As such, skiboards provide a real opportunity to instigate these paradigm shifts.

I believe that we were meant to engage our deeper potentialities in life. Instead of settling for mediocre, we're here to extend ourselves, to pursue magnificence. Pushing the limits of performance is a prerequisite condition for not only the experience of the Zone during skiing, but for entering into a more expanded sense of self and waking up from the trance of cultural conditioning. To live an extraordinary life is why we're here.

We can absolutely transcend biological and cultural determinants. Pushing past what has been done before, taking a risk and living on the edge, may in the end, not only allow us to break out of the confines of existing paradigms, of sub-optimal functioning, but will open us up to a whole new world of unimagined possibilities.

Skiboarding is a direct means for self-actualizing, for defying the forces of conditioning and inertia. It present us with the opportunity to develop to our full potential. It's this deeper calling within, to be the best that we can be, to express our true magnificence that I believe urges us to explore a whole new adventure, such as skiboarding.

CHAPTER 12

The Best Kept Secret

*Our normal waking consciousness, rational consciousness as
we call it, is but one special type of consciousness,
while all about it, parted from it by the filmiest of screens,
there lie potential forms of consciousness entirely different.
We may go through life without suspecting their existence,
but apply the requisite stimulus, and at a touch they are there
in all their completeness. No account of the universe in its
totality can be final which leaves these other forms of
consciousness quite disregarded.*
- William James -

Self-Actualization and the Zone

There's more to just experiencing peak moments on the slopes.
What I've found is that skiboards also set the stage for self-
actualization. In culturing the art of letting go and being fully
present with our attention to the moment, not only our skills
improve, but a broader personal transformation takes place.
While certainly many active sports produce these opportune
moments that break us free, I find that skiboards in particular,
really deliver, and fast!

Numerous studies document positive benefits for those who
regularly experience the Zone. Schwartz, in studies of athletes,
concludes, "Those who experience these moments are forever
changed. They then seek to recreate the feelings of exquisite joy
this state of flow engenders. They push to work at the upper limits
of their abilities." Supportive research adds that regular peak
moments result in greater stress reduction, positive emotional and
psychological health characteristics in life and greater immunity
to disease. (Anise; Anise; Blanchard; Castillo; Chaudhuri; Gifford-
May & Thompson; Greeley & McCready; Hardy; Hoover; Laski;
Livingston; MacKinnon; Maslow; Osborne; Rahilly; Roberts;

Sheehy; Spilka et al.; Tart; Thomas & Cooper; Torrence; Vaughan; Wangle; Wells; Whalen & Csikszentmihalyi; White; Wilber; Wuthnow)

An interviewee offers his experience:

I think my health both physically and mentally has improved. Just the memory of the zone makes me feel better. I have an attitude reinforced by those experiences of confidence. This carries over. I notice that I have a heightened level of commitment which I attribute to the Zone also. (Jeff)

Yet, this is the really good part. There is a host of supporting evidence demonstrating that regular 'peakers', besides the positive effects discussed above regarding peak experiences, also experience more permanent life changes as a result of these moments. Research with thousands and thousands of subjects demonstrate that individuals who have regular peak experiences not only transcend the usual constraints of consensus trance, but tap into an expanded, actualized state of consciousness (as Maslow has suggested).

This expanded state happens certainly on the slopes, but the effects of this paradigm shift also tend to persist, carrying over into our everyday life. Peakers are more capable of easily and consistently overcoming the inhibitions that typically block the expression of their greater human potential in all areas of life. (Bucke; Castillo; Csikszentmihalyi; Frankl; Greeley & McCready; Hardy; Hebb; James; Jung; Kobasha et al; Laski; May; McClain & Andrews; Osborne; Perls; Quarrick; Ravizza; Rogers; Sheehy, Spilka et al; Tart; Thomas & Cooper; Underhill; White)

One co-researcher offers this:

What I experience is serious happiness. More relaxation physically. Feel more secure about dealing with life. Problems that seemed mountains before are molehills now. I would think that I would be more of a negative, depressed and skeptical person if I didn't have regular bouts of being in the Zone. (Mary)

These moments of flow or being in the Zone allow us to glimpse our own magnificent possibilities. Our Authentic Self, often buried beneath layers and layers of cultural conditioning, can now shine forth. Awareness is heightened and expanded, no longer inhibited and deadened by paradigm paralysis, and a range of new possibilities and abilities begin to dawn.

Studies into self-actualizing individuals confirm this. Self-actualizers have been found to more easily focus their attention at will, rather than having it continually inaccessible and unconsciously controlled by cultural conditioning. They're simply more able to regain control of their attention from 'attention drift'. The more they 'practice' breaking free of conditioning, through moments of absorbed attention, the more skilled they are at breaking free in all areas of life. (Csikszentmihalyi; Maslow; Quarrick) This sets the stage for living more fulfilling and extraordinary lives, the domain of self-actualizers.

One skiboarder states:

I could never go back and do things I used to do, like have dead end jobs. I could never do that, I could never shrink myself down that way. I'm too big, I know I'm bigger than that because I had the experience – this vibrational upliftment, tuned into something greater than the normal everyday workday. I just feel like I've touched something in myself that lifts me above and out of my everyday life, but yet confirms the best part of me. I feel like I was dead until I discovered the Zone. (John)

In my doctoral dissertation, I found that the individuals I studied, who were regularly experiencing the Zone (for more than five years), also scored higher on ratings of self-actualization in life. In other words, there was a direct connection between frequency of peak experiences precipitated when engaged in active sports, such as skiboarding (the focus of my research) and the actualization of one's greater human potential. (Roberts) This was a real eye opener for me and I believe important knowledge for my readers as well.

The conclusion of my dissertation, and this was also based on a comprehensive investigation of all the relevant literature, is that when we can experience moments of peak performance on a regular basis, the overall quality of our life will dramatically improve. We'll begin to function at optimal levels (beyond the average) in all areas of our life, not only on the slopes. I of course don't expect you to just believe me. Have an adventure and find out for yourself. *The proof is in the pudding!* It's an odd phrase, but you get the idea.

In the literature, major similarities to the characteristics of Maslow's self-actualizers are found in Allport's mature personality, Amabile's notion of intrinsic motivation, Bandura's theory of effectance motivation, Csikszentmihalyi's autotelic personality, deCharms' concept of personal causation, Deci and Ryan's ideas on autonomy, Frankl's self-transcendent person, Fromm's productive personality, Gowan's creative individual, Hebb's research in optimal arousal, Jung's individuated person, studies of hardiness (Kobasha et al.; Kobasha), Roger's becoming person, Sheehy's authentic personality, and White's notion of competence. This extensive body of research focuses on those individuals who represent the best and healthiest human specimens, believed to be fully functioning. All of these investigators associate the regular occurrence of peak moments as being the primary cause for this optimal functioning above the norm.

There is much evidence pointing to the understanding that regular exposure to transcending the Conditioned Self may initiate a more permanent lifetime paradigm shift. Imagine just cruising down the slopes on skiboards free as a bird, enjoying the full experience of uninhibited flow, while at the same time, upgrading our overall life experience. Skiboarding allows us to live to our greater human potential. Wow, what a secret that is!

As a result of regular paradigm shifting on the slopes, we'll begin to exhibit certain perceptual, psychological and even physiological changes. Probably good to know what we're all in for, so following is a list of the associated characteristics of self-actualizing or fully functioning individuals (based on extensive research) who are quite naturally frequent 'peakers':

1. Heightened, expanded and more accurate perception of reality; accompanied by greater clarity with an enhanced objectivity.
2. Increased acceptance of self and others, including strengths and shortcomings, without complaint or worry.
3. Increased spontaneity, naturalness and simplicity.
4. Alignment with a mission or calling, doing work we truly enjoy, that brings out our greatest talents.
5. Becoming more individuated, being our own person, free from the need for approval from others.
6. A sense of sacredness and gratitude.
7. Greater freshness of appreciation and the ability to enjoy life, with enhanced wonder and awe; decreased tendency to take life for granted or become bored.
8. Higher frequency of peak experiences on a regular basis and in many situations.
9. Feeling a greater kinship with humanity with greater compassion, empathy and stronger interest in the welfare of others.
10. Increased capacity for intimate relationships with friends, family and significant others.
11. Greater tolerance and acceptance of others.
12. Enjoy the sheer act of doing, as much or more than achieving the goal; i.e. enjoying the journey even more than the destination.
13. Greater sense of humor.
14. More creative, original, and innovative.
15. Natural resistance to enculturation and the social pressures to conform, fit in, and follow the rules.
16. Ability to be firmly rooted in the present moment and less influenced by past determinants or future projections.
17. Change in our worldview towards greater well-being, joyfulness and harmony; seeing the good in life.
18. More enjoyment of challenges, even problems, new experiences and the ability to find excitement in life.
19. A loss of fear, anxiety, inhibition, defense, confusion, and restraint.
20. Deeply felt pervasive positive mood – joy, ecstasy, exaltation and love.

21. Ineffability – frequent claims that language is inadequate to describe what is happening.
22. Experiences of 'unitive consciousness', a feeling of oneness with all things.

Of course, these characteristics are similar to the characteristics of peak experiences mentioned earlier. The difference however, is that these experiences during peak moments of performance have crystallized and carried over into everyday life. A more permanent shift has occurred with the regular exposure to deautomatization.

As Arleen describes:

The most positive thing that I get from this is the ability to shift my awarenesses and thinking so that when I am in everyday life, I don't get stuck. I don't get stuck in ideologies that can pin and enslave me or of perceptions that can pin or enslave me. I think being in the Zone gives me the ability to move out of those traps much more easily. I also notice that I have a younger attitude. An ability to look at things in fresh ways.

Yet, these changes are not even the whole story. The whole story is still being written by every one of us! Who really knows what a person living to their full potential can achieve and experience in life? It's rarely contemplated in our culture. I do know however that living to our full potential (more than the 3-5% it's estimated most people use) means experiencing greater success, joy, creativity, love, vitality and aliveness. Research supports this contention.

Awakening

There is an overall expanded awareness, but I've been with it
so long that I don't notice it anymore. It's who I am now. My
awareness is expanded through experiencing the Zone. Try to
bring it up in regular conversation and most people would see
you as off center. No, you guys are all off center.
Centered is the place!
- Brad -

Throughout human history, psychologists, scientists, poets, philosophers, religious leaders and spiritual teachers have continually portrayed the normal waking state of consciousness as being, in actuality, more a state of sleep than wakefulness. They've concluded that the majority of human beings are really living in an entranced, mechanical, dispirited state of existence.

Our normal waking state has been referred to as a state of "automatization" (Deikman), "living in a dream world" or being in a "cultural trance" (Ferguson), described as "spiritual atrophy" (Deutsch),"consensus trance" (Tart), "mindlessness" (Langer; Rinpoche), being "asleep" (Ouspensky), "verbal trance" (Perls), "automaton conformity" (Fromm), "inauthenticity" (Sheehy), being "bound" (Wilber) and the "business of living consciousness" (Quarrick), to name a few. Though in waking consciousness, seeming to be awake, the average human being is viewed as being quite deadened to the experience of their own life, having lost touch not only with their life, but also with their Authentic Self. Further, there is no recognition that they're asleep and engaging in only a small fraction of their possible potential to experience life.

In contrast to achieving authentic growth, most individuals in our culture live behind a facade, hypnotized into perceiving not what is, but what has been conditioned by society, living most of the time in the past or future, and rarely in the present moment. This facade that we've been taught to most identify with, I've referred to as the Conditioned Self. As the Conditioned Self gains dominance over our attention, we become more alienated from our Authentic Self. (Adler; Fairbairn; Goffman; Horney;

Jourard; Jung; Kierkegaard; Laing; Rogers) This was touched upon in our previous discussion of paradigm paralysis.

Ouspensky, perhaps the most prolific of teachers on this subject, as well as a recognized mathematician, quotes his teacher Gurdieff:

Man's possibilities are very great. You cannot conceive even a shadow of what man is capable of attaining. But nothing can be attained in sleep. In the consciousness of a sleeping man his illusions, his 'dreams' are mixed with reality. He lives in a subjective world and he can never escape from it. And this is the reason why he can never make use of all the powers he possesses and why he always lives in only a small part of himself. He lives in sleep all his life and he dies in sleep.

Ouspensky refers to this unconscious and automatic tendency as living out of the Conditioned Self. We're each born as self-aware and authentic beings, experiencing what it is to be awake, to be developing towards our unique potential. However, that possibility begins to quickly disappear even in childhood as a result of powerful cultural conditioning.

Many investigators in this field have determined that it's the repeated experiencing of the Authentic Self that continues to weaken the constrictions of paradigm paralysis. We then are able to access and express more of our human potentialities and achieve a higher state of optimum functioning. (De Ropp; Osborne; Ouspensky; Rinpoche; Roshi; Tart; Underhill; Watts; Wilber) It's these peak moments that provide direct experience of our essential being that was previously confined behind enculturation.

All co-researchers in my study experienced ego-transcendence and the awakening of the Authentic Self during moments of being in the Zone. Comments from these individuals such as 'dropping all limits and masks,' 'an awakening,' 'being who you are,' 'cosmic consciousness,' 'being or essence,' and an 'actualized sense of self' confirmed they were having similar experiences to other research findings. My conclusion was that they became deautomatized from conditioned thought patterns and consensus trance.

What results during a peak performance experience is a figure-ground reversal. That which was in the background of awareness, the Authentic Self, moves to the foreground of awareness, while the ego or Conditioned Self is transcended. This is a common transformation when the circumstances are right. (James; Maslow; Csikszentmihalyi; Quarrick) The paradigm shift is not just into a sense of liberation and creative expression, for example on the slopes, but the shift has even more significant implications for us regular 'peakers.'

This "intense, single-minded attention state" (Quarrick), achieved through various physical activities such as skiboarding and other means (assuming the necessary prerequisites are met) has been proposed to be a path to self-realization in the Eastern sense, breaking through the facade or illusion of the ego. Research strongly suggests that these brief awakenings from the limited state of awareness experienced during these peak moments solidify into a more encompassing awake state of consciousness. (Bucke; Franz; Jung; Koplowitz; Krishnamurti; Ouspensky; Quarrick; Tart; Underhill; Vaughan; Walsh; Wilber; Zukav) All co-researchers in my study attested to this awakening to a more real self as well. They also were found to demonstrate higher scores on self-actualization characteristics indicating that there was indeed carry over in these effects into everyday life. (Roberts) Most of these co-researchers had been having regular experiences of the zone for five years or longer.

As discussed, during peak moments of performance, the paralysis of paradigms or Conditioned Self slip to the background of consciousness, and what was in the background, the true or Authentic Self comes to the foreground of perception. This direct experience of the Authentic Self has been identified by numerous researchers to be a distinct fourth state of consciousness, with its own unique physiological and psychological characteristics. (Alexander et al.; Bucke; Deikman; Ferguson; Quarrick; Welwood) This state of consciousness is different from the other three states of waking, sleeping and dreaming.

As the distinction between experiencer and the experience disappears, this fourth state of consciousness emerges. (Alexander et al.; Castillo; Csikszentmihalyi; Deikman; DeRopp; Dillbeck & Alexander; Farrow; Ferguson; Levine; Tart; Vaughan; Walsh & Vaughan; Welwood; White; Wilber) This intensified wakefulness has been found to show consistent descriptions from independent subjects across many different studies as well as demonstrating physiological distinctions as compared to normal states of consciousness, based on brain wave measurements as well as other measures.

Similar descriptions to this fourth state of consciousness have also been found in the experiences of Zen masters, Yogis, Sufis, Christian mystics and Native American Shamans. As mentioned above, what's amazing is that the same characteristics of this state of consciousness have been identified in athletes during peak performance moments as well. (Csikszentmihalyi; Murphy) All research seems to verify this fourth state as not only distinct, but also readily accessible given the right prerequisites.

In a pioneering biographical study of exemplary models of fully functioning individuals, Richard Bucke, M. D., postulated the existence of this higher or fourth state of consciousness. He called it "cosmic consciousness." This new faculty, an expanded state of universal consciousness, he found from his studies, to occur in the best human specimens and at those times when they were functioning at their best. He believed that regular exposure to this experience of cosmic consciousness would begin to stabilize this higher state of consciousness on a more permanent basis. Individuals, functioning at their best, definitely fits the descriptions and characteristics of peak experiences.

Reviewing case studies concerning experiences of this expanded state of awareness, Gary Zukav reports, "The individual comes to feel, beyond any shadow of a doubt, that he is fundamentally one with the entire universe. His sense of identity expands far beyond the narrow confines of his mind and body and embraces the entire cosmos." He and others view this expansion of identity, of who we are, to represent an advanced state of consciousness that is emerging in our culture. (Bucke; James; Maslow; Quarrick)

The characteristics of this expanded state of liberation, of self-actualization, are quite similar to those of higher mystical states as described throughout the history of the world. Similar descriptions, for example, can be found in the teachings of all the major world religions, including Hinduism, Buddhism, Christianity, Taoism, Judaism, as well as various 'new age' teachings. (Brother David; Bucke; Castillo; Ferguson; Gifford-May & Thompson; Grof; Huxley; James; Kabat-Zinn; Laski; Vaughan; White; Wilber; Yogananda; Zukav) There is a consistency in the descriptions of this state of consciousness across many teachings adding further proof for its existence.

Maslow states, "It may turn out that only peakers can achieve full identity." He believes that the path to self-realization, ego-transcendence and liberation lies in the continued experiencing of the True Self that peak experiences afford. This I find fascinating. In other words, if we're truly to live our life to the fullest and become the person we were born to be, we must experience these peak moments on a frequent basis. Even better, this path of unfolding is one of joy, not suffering!

Sports, and skiing more specifically, are perfect in this sense. They allow for a total concentration of attention, while at the same time, a full letting go into the present moment. It invites us to challenge ourselves and push the limits of performance. These mini-transformations in the Zone occur of course after mastering the equipment and skills of our particular sport. In short, expanded awareness, while being physically active, and challenging ourselves, creates the exact circumstances for awakening from cultural trance on a more permanent basis!

One skiboarder wrote in:

It becomes easier to awaken each time and in other life situations. (Tom)

Peak experiences represent a brief exposure to what it is to be self-realized and a fully awake and fully alive human being. These moments of instant joy offer glimpses into our true being behind the facade of the Conditioned Self. Further, the regular exposure to these transcendent moments leads to the enhanced unfolding of our true potential, stabilizing this more expanded, fourth state of consciousness.

Whether called self-realization, enlightenment, self-actualization, optimal functioning or simply just feeling more alive, something profound shifts when we're experiencing these peak moments of joy on a regular basis. Am I saying that we can become enlightened if we ride skiboards – who knows! That's for each of us to discover. Research however does support this very contention. (Alexander et al.; Bucke; Csikszentmihalyi; Deikman; DeRopp; Dillbeck & Alexander; Franz; Grof; Hay; James; Jung; Koplowitz; Laski; Maslow; Mathes et al.; Murphy; Pahnke; Quarrick; Tart; Thomas & Cooper; Underhill; Vaughan; Walsh & Vaughan; White; Young; Zukav)

"Honey, I need to go skiboarding today. I have to become all I can be!"

For centuries, traditional methods of meditation, mindfulness practice and other spiritual techniques have been used to accelerate the unfolding of Self-Realization. I find based on my own research with skiboarders, as well as other active sports, that being in physical action quickens the speed of these breakthroughs. It takes us out of our heads and puts us directly into the action, causing us to be fully embodied in the be-here-now moment. Besides enhancing the joy, pushing the limits accelerates the onset of these peak experiences. Research points out that the more exposure to these moments, the more life transforms in a positive direction.

One co-researcher offers this comment:

You have to have some kind of concentration, a grounding, to be in the Zone. Once you identify it, then you can find different ways of entering into it in other areas of your life. (Aaron)

While skiboards prove to be a powerful means for learning to ski instantly, what I feel is even more important is that they represent a new approach to self-actualization and blossoming into the person we were truly born to be. It's this that we all can discover for ourselves. Best of all, we don't really need to do anything special, other than ride as often as we can and have a great time.

Instant Skiing, Instant Fun is ultimately about this personal transformation on the slopes. However, though it starts on the mountain, very soon it opens up a whole new world of possibilities. The key principles of breakthrough that apply to improving our skiing skills will also bring joy to our souls and enrich our lives in unimagined ways. See you on the slopes!

We rarely experience times when we're fully alive and awake to the here-and-now real moments in our lives. Skiing provides this opportunity to awaken from consensus trance and regain the joy of being fully alive. To me, riding skiboards in particular is the same as making our life extraordinary. It's like a concentrated course in self-actualization.

Whether it's skiing, or any other area of your life, why not experience all the joy, thrill and aliveness that you can?

This is really the only life truly worth living.
                          - Doc Roberts –

Bibliographical References

Aanstoos, R. "A Brief History of the Human Science Research Conference." *Journal of Humanistic Psychology*, 1990, 30(3): 137-45.

Abelson, R. "Psychological Status of the Script Concept." *American Psychologist,* 1981, 36: 715-29.

Adler, Alfred. *The Individual Psychology of Alfred Adler: A Systematic Presentation in Selections from His Writings.* H. L. Ansbacher and R. R. Ansbacher (Eds.). New York: Harper, 1956.

Adler, N. *The Underground Stream: New Life Styles and the Antinomian Personality.* New York: Harper and Row, 1972.

Alexander, C., et al. "Growth of Higher Stages of Consciousness". In *Higher Stages of Human Development,* Eds. C. Alexander and E. Langer. New York: Oxford University Press, 1991.

Allport, G. *Becoming: Basic Considerations for a Psychology of Personality.* New Haven: Yale University Press, 1955.

Allport, G. *Pattern and Growth in Personality.* New York: Holt, Rinehart & Winston, 1961.

Altschuler, Richard and N. Regush. *Open Reality: The Way Out of Mimicking Happiness.* New York: G. P. Putnam's Sons, 1974.

Amabile, T. M. *The Social Psychology of Creativity.* New York: Springer-Verlag, 1983.

Apter, M. J. *The Dangerous Edge: The Psychology of Excitement.* New York: The Free Press, 1992.

Assagioli, Roberto. *Psychosynthesis*. New York: Penguin Books, 1976.

Aurobindo, Sri. *On Physical Education*. Pondichery, India: Sri Aurobindo Ashram Publications.

Baldwin, James. *Nobody Knows My Name*. New York: Dial Press, 1961.

Bandura, A. "Self-efficacy: Toward a Unifying Theory of Behavioral Change." *Psychological Review*, 1977, 84: 191-215.

Blanchard, W. "Psychodynamic Aspects of the Peak Experience." *Psychoanalytic Review*, 1969, 56 (1): 87-112.

Braga, Joseph and Laurie Braga, Foreword to *Death: The Final Stage of Growth,* by Kubler-Ross, Elisabeth. Englewood Cliffs, N.J.: Prentice Hall, 1975.

Bruner, J.S. "Personality Dynamics and the Process of Perceiving." In *Perception: An Approach to Personality*. Eds. R. R. Blake and G.V. Ransey. New York: Ronald, 1951.

Brenneche, John and Robert G. Amich. *Significance: The Struggle We Share*. 2nd Ed. Beverly Hills, CA: Benziger, Bruce, and Glencoe, 1975.

Brother David. "Fully Alive: A Peak Experience with a Modern Mystic." In *Spirituality and Health*, Preview Issue, Fall 1996: 6-8.

Bucke, M. *Cosmic Consciousness*. New York: E. P. Dutton, 1969.

Bush, Gregory. *Lord of Attention: The Crowd Metaphor in Industrializing America*. Amherst: University of Massachusetts Press, 1991.

Callaway, Enoch and George Stone, "Re-Evaluating Focus of Attention." In *Drugs and Behavior*, Ed. Leonard Uhr and James G. Miller. New York: Wiley, 1960.

Campbell, Joseph. *The Power of Myth*. New York: Doubleday, 1988.

Castillo, R. "The Transpersonal Psychology of Patanjali's Yoga Sutra. (Book I: Samadhi): A Translation and Interpretation." *Journal of Mind and Behavior*, 1985, 6 (3): 391-417.

Chaudhuri, H. "Psychology: Humanistic and Transpersonal." *Journal of Humanistic Psychology*, 1975, 15: 7-15.

Chuang Wu-tzu. Translated by Burton Watson. In *The Enlightened Mind: An Anthology of Sacred Prose*. Stephen Mitchell (Ed.), New York: Harper Collins, 1991.

Chuang Wu-tzu. *The Complete Works of Chuang-tzu*. Translated by Burton Watson. New York: Columbia University Press, 1968.

Cohen, R. *Neurophysiology of Attention*. New York: Plenum Press, 1955.

Csikszentmihalyi, Mihaly. *Flow: The Psychology of Optimal Experience*. New York: Harper Perennial, 1990.

Csikszentmihalyi, Mihaly & I. S. Csikszentmihalyi. Eds. *Optimal Experience: Psychological Studies in the Flow of Consciousness*. New York: Cambridge University Press, 1988.

Csikszentmihalyi, Mihaly. *The Evolving Self: A Psychology for the Third Millennium*. New York: Harper Collins, 1993.

Csikszentmihalyi, Mihaly and Eugen Rochberg-Halton. *The Meaning of Things*. Cambridge: Cambridge University Press, 1981.

Csikszentmihalyi, Mihaly, K. Rathunde, and S. Whalen. *Talented Teenagers: A Longitudinal Study of their Development*. New York: Cambridge University Press, 1993

Dawkins, R. *The Extended Phenotype*. Oxford: Oxford University Press, 1982.

DeBerry, Stephen. *The Externalization of Consciousness and the Psychopathology of Everyday Life*. New York: Greenwood Press, 1991.

DeCharms, R. *Personal Causation: The Internal Affective Determinants of Behavior*. New York: Academic Press, 1968.

Deci, E. L. and R. M. Ryan. *Intrinsic Motivation and Self-Determination in Human Behavior*. New York: Plenum Press, 1985.

Deikman, Arthur. "Experimental Meditation." *Journal of Nervous Mental Disorders,* 1963, 136: 329-343.

Deikman, Arthur. *Personal Freedom: On Finding Your Way to the Real World*. New York: Grossman Publishers, 1976.

Deikman, Arthur. "De-Automatization and the Mystic Experience." *Psychiatry*, 1966, 29: 329-343.

De Ropp, Robert. *The Master Game*. New York: Delacorte Press, 1968.

Deutsch, Eliot. *Personhood, Creativity and Freedom*. Honolulu: University of Hawaii Press, 1982.

Dewey, John. "Having An Experience." (1934) In *A Modern Book of Esthetics: An Anthology*, Ed. Melvin Rader. New York: Holt, Rinehart and Winston, 1979.

Dillbeck, M. and C. Alexander. "Higher States of Consciousness: Maharishi Mahesh Yogi's Vedic Psychology of Human Development." *Journal of Mind & Behavior,* 1989, 10 (4): 307-34.

Dhiravamsa. *The Way of Non-Attachment: The Practice of Insight Meditation.* Wellingborough, Northamptonshire: Turnstone Press, 1984.

Donner, E. and M. Csikzentmihalyi. "Transforming Stress to Flow." *Executive Excellence,* 1992, 9 (2): 16-18.

Eidelberg, Ludwig. Ed. *Encyclopedia of Psychoanalysis.* New York: Collier-McMillan Free Press, 1968.

Ellenberger, Henrie. *The Discovery of the Unconscious.* New York: Basic Books, 1970.

Easterbrook, J. "The Effect of the Cue Utilization and the Organization of Behavior." Psychological Review 1959, 66: 183-201.

Fairbairn, W. *Psychoanalytic Studies of the Personality.* London: Tavistock, 1952.

Farrow, J. "Physiological Changes Associated with Trans-cendental Consciousness." *Scientific Research on the Transcendental Meditation Program: Collected Papers,* Ed. D. Orme-Johnson and J. Farrow. 1976, 1: 108-33.

Ferguson, Marilyn. *The Aquarian Conspiracy.* Los Angeles: J. P. Tarcher, 1980.

Fiske, D. W., and S. R. Maddi, Eds. *Functions of Varied Experience.* Homewood, Ill.: Dorsey Press, 1961.

Frankl, Viktor. *Man's Search for Meaning: An Introduction to Logotherapy,* 2nd Ed. Boston: Beacon Press, 1962.

Franz, M. "The Process of Individuation." In *Man and His Symbols*, Ed. C. Jung. New York: Doubleday, 1964.

Fromm, Erich. *Escape from Freedom*. New York: Avon Books, 1941.

Fromm, Erich. *Man for Himself*. New York: Holt, Rinehart and Winston, 1947.

Gallwey, Timothy W. *The Inner Game of Tennis*. New York: Random House, 1974.

Gifford-May, D. and N. Thompson. "Deep States of Meditation: Phenomenological Reports of Experience." *Journal of Transpersonal Psychology*, 1994, 26 (2): 117-38.

Gill, M. and M. Brenman. *Hypnosis and Related States: Psychoanalytic Studies in Regression*. New York: International Universities Press, 1959.

Giogi, G. *Psychology as a Human Science: A Phenomenologically Based Approach*. New York: Harper & Row, 1970.

Goffman, Erving. *The Presentation of Self in Everyday Life*. New York: Doubleday, 1959.

Goldstein, J. *The Experience of Insight: A Simple and Direct Guide to Buddhist Meditation*. Boston: Shambhala Publications, 1987.

Goldstein, J. and J. Kornfield. *Seeking the Heart of Wisdom: The Path of Insight Meditation*. Boston: Shambhala Publications, 1987.

Gowan, J. C. *The Development of the Creative Individual*. San Diego: Robert Knapp, 1972.

Greeley, Andrew and William McCready. Published in *New York Times Magazine*, January 16, 1975.

Grof, S. *The Adventure of Self-Exploration*. Albany, NY: SUNY Press, 1987.

Hardy, A. *Spiritual Nature of Man*. Oxford: Clarendon Press, 1979.

Hay, D. *Exploring Inner Space: Scientists and Religious Experience*. Harmondsworth, England: Penguin, 1982.

Harmon, William. "Old Wine in New Wineskins." In *Challenges of Humanistic Psychology*, Ed. J. Bugenthal. New York: McGraw Hill, 1962.

Hartmann, H. *Ego Psychology and the Problem of Adaptation*. New York: International Universities, 1958.

Hay, D. *Exploring Inner Space: Scientists and Religious Experience*. Harmondsworth, England: Penguin Books, 1982.

Hebb, D. O. "Drive and the CNS." *Psychological Review*, 1955, July: 243-52.

Hebb, D.O. *A Textbook in Psychology*. Philadelphia: W. B. Saunders, 1958.

Herrigel, Eugen. *Zen and the Art of Archery*. New York: Random House/Vintage, 1953.

Hoover, T. "Skydivers: Speculations of Psychodynamics." In *Perceptual and Motor Skills*, 1978, 47: 629-30.

Horney, Karen. *Neurosis and Human Growth*. New York: W. W. Norton, 1950.

Hudson, Frederic M. *The Adult Years: Mastering the Art of Self-Renewal*. San Francisco: Jossey-Bass Publishers, 1991.

Huxley, A. "The Visionary Experience." In *The Highest State of Consciousness*, Ed. John White. New York: Doubleday, 1972.

James, William. *The Principles of Psychology*. Vol. 1. New York: Henry Holt and Co., 1890.

James, William. "The Energies of Men." In *The Moral Equivalent to War and Other Essays*. Ed. John K. Roth. New York: Harper & Row, 1971.

James, William. "The World We Live In." *The Philosophy of William James*. New York: Modern Library, 1953.

James, William. *The Varieties of Religious Experience*. New York: New American Library, 1958.

Jaynes, Julian. *The Origin of Consciousness in the Breakdown of the Bicameral Mind*. Boston: Houghton Mifflin Co., 1976.

Jourard, Sidney. *The Transparent Self*. New York: Van Nostrand, 1971.

Jung, C. G. *Two Essays on Analytical Psychology*. New York: Pantheon, 1953.

Jung, C. G. *The Archetypes and the Collective Unconscious*. In Vol. 91 of *The Collected Works of C. G. Jung*. Princeton, N. J.: Princeton University Press, 1959.

Kabat-Zinn, J. *Wherever You Go There You Are*. New York: Hyperion, 1994.

Kane, Michael. "Radical In-Line." In *the Boulder Planet*. July 10, 1996, First Ed.

Kasamatsu, Akira and Tomio Hirai. "An Electroencephalographic Study on the Zen Meditation (Zazen)." in *Altered States of Consciousness,* Ed. Charles Tart. New York: Wiley, 1969.

Kaydin, A. "Drawing Valid Inferences from Case Studies." *Journal of Consulting and Clinical Psychology*, 1981, 49(2): 183-92.

Keene, Sam. *Hymns to An Unknown God*. New York: Bantam Books, 1994.

Kierkegaard, S. *The Sickness Unto Death*. Trans. W. Lowrie. New York: Doubleday, 1954.

Koestler, Arthur. *The Act of Creation*. New York: Macmillan, 1964.

Kobasha, S., Maddi, S. and S. Kahn. "Hardiness and Health: A Prospective Study." *Journal of Personality and Social Psychology*, 1982, 42: 168-177.

Kobasha, S. and M. Puccetti. "Personality and Exercise as Buffers in the Stress-Illness." *Journal of Behavioral Medicine*, 1982, 5: 391-404.

Koplowitz, H. "Unitary Operational Thinking." In *Brain/Mind Bulletin*, 1978): 48.

Korchin, S. J. "Anxiety and Cognition." In *Cognition: Theory, Research and Promise*. Ed. C. Scheerer. New York: Harper and Row, 1964.

Kornfield, J. and P. Breiter. *A Still Forest Pool: The Insight Meditation of Achaan Chah*. Wheaton, Illinois: The Theosophical Publishing House, 1985.

Krishnamurti, J. *The First and Last Freedom*. New York: Harper and Row, 1954.

Kubler-Ross, Elisabeth. *Death: The Final Stage of Growth*. Englewood Cliffs, N. J.: Prentice Hall, 1975.

Kuhn, Thomas. *The Structure of Scientific Revolutions*. Chicago, Ill.: University of Chicago Press, 1962.

Kwee, M. Ed. *Psychotherapy, Meditation and Health*. London: East-West, 1990.

Laing, R. *The Politics of Experience*. New York: Ballantine Books, 1967.

Langer, Ellen. *Mindfulness*. Reading, Mass.: University Press, 1989.

Langer, E. and L. Imber. "When Practice Makes Imperfect: The Debilitating Effects of Overlearning." *Journal of Personality and Social Psychology*, 1979, 37: 2014-25.

Lasch, Christoper. *The Minimal Self*. New York: Norton, 1984.

Laski, M. *Ecstasy: A Study of Some Secular and Religious Experiences*. New York: Greenwood Press, 1968.

LeShan, Lawrence. *Alternate Realities: The Search for the Full Human Being*. New York: M. Evans and Co., 1976.

Levine, P., Herbert, J., Haynes, C. and U. Stroebel. "EEG Coherence During the Transcendental Meditation Technique." *Scientific Research on the Transcendental Meditation Program: Collected Papers*, Ed. D. Orme-Johnson and J. Farrow. 1977, 1: 187-207.

Lezak, Muriel D. *Neuropsychological Assessment*. New York: Oxford University Press, 1983.

Lindsley, Donald B. "Physiological Psychology." *Annual Review of Psychology,* 1956, 7: 323-48.

Livingston, D. "Transcendental States of Consciousness and the Healthy Personality: An Overview." Ph.D. Dissertation. University of Arizona, 1975.

Lowen, A. *The Betrayal of the Body*. New York: MacMillan Co., 1967.

Luce, G. "Western Psychology meets Tibetan Buddhism." *Crystal Mirror*, 1974, 3: 49-75.

MacKinnon, D. "The Highly Effective Individual." *Teachers College Record*, 1960, 61: 367-68

Marrone, R. *Body of Knowledge: An Introduction to Body/Mind Psychology*. New York: SUNY Press, 1990.

Maslow, Abraham. *Eupsychian Management: A Journal*. Homewood, Ill.: Irwin-Dorsey, 1965.

Maslow, Abraham. *Psychology of Science*. New York: Harper & Row, 1966.

Maslow, Abraham. *The Farther Reaches of Human Nature*. Penguin Books, 1971.

Maslow, Abraham. *Religions, Values, and Peak-Experiences*. New York: Penguin Books, 1970.

Maslow, Abraham. *Toward a Psychology of Being*. New York: Van Nostrand Reinhold, 1968.

Masterson, J. F. *The Real Self*. New York: Brunner/Mazel, 1985.

Mathes, E., Zevon, M., Roter, P., and S. Joerger. "Peak Experience Tendencies: Scale Development and Theory." *Journal of Humanistic Psychology*, 1982, 22 (3): 92-108

May, Rollo. *The Courage to Create*. New York: Bantam Books, 1975.

McClain, E. and H. Andrews. "Some Personality Correlates of Peak Experiences: A Study in Self-Actualization." Journal of Clinical Psychology, 1969, 25 (1): 36-38.

McClelland, D.C. and Liberman, A. M. "The Effect of Need for Achievement on Recognition of Need-Related Words." *Journal of Personality,* 1949, 18: 236-251.

McClintock, M. K. "A Functional Approach to the Behavioral Endocrinology of Rodents." In *Psychobiology of Reproduction*, Ed. D. Crews, 176-203. Englewood Cliffs, N.J.: Prentice-Hall, 1987.

McClintock, M. K. "Innate Behavior is Not Innate: A Biosocial Perspective on Parenting." *Signs,* 1979, 4(4): 703-10.

Murphy, Gardner. *Personality: A Biosocial Approach to Origins and Structure.* New York: Harper, 1947.

Murphy, Michael. "Sport as Yoga." *Journal of Humanistic Psychology*, Fall, 1977, 17 (4): 21-33.

Murphy, M., and Donovan, S. *The Physical and Psychological Effects of Meditation.* San Rafael, CA: Esalen Institute, 1988.

Naranja, C. *The One Quest.* New York: Viking Press, 1972.

Nideffer, Robert. *The Inner Athlete.* New York: Crowell, 1976.

Noble, K. "Psychological Health and Experience of Transcendence." *Consulting Psychologist*, 1987, 15 (4): 601-14.

Nyanaponika, M. "The Power of Mindfulness." In *Pathways of Buddhist Thought*, Ed. N. Mahathera. New York: Barnes and Noble, 1971.

Osborne, Arthur. *The Collected Works of Ramana Maharshi.* London: Rider, 1959.

Ouspensky, P. D. *In Search of the Miraculous.* Orlando, Florida: Harcourt Brace Jovanovich, 1949.

Pahnke,W. "LSD and Religious Experience." In *LSD, Man and Society*, Ed. R. Debold and R. Leaf. Middletown, CT.: Wesleyan University Press, 1967.

Pahnke, W. and W. Richards. Quoted in J. Heaney Ed., *Psyche and Spirit* (pp. 109-118). New York: Paulist Press, 1973.

Pearce, J. *Magical Child*. New York: Penguin Group, 1992.

Perls, Fritz. *Gestalt Therapy Verbatim*. Lafeyette, CA: Real People Press, 1969.

Piaget, Jean. *The Construction of Reality in the Child*. New York: Basic, 1954.

Powell, John. *Fully Human, Fully Alive*. Allen, Texas: Tabor Publishing, 1976.

Prather, Hugh. *Notes on How to Live in the World . . . and Still Be Happy*. New York: Doubleday, 1986.

Pratto, Felicia. "Consciousness and Automatic Evaluation." In *The Heart's Eye: Emotional Influences in Perception and Attention*. Eds. Niedenthal, Paula M. and Shinobu Kitayama. San Diego: Academic Press, 1994.

Prince, R. "Mystical States and the Concept of Regression." *Psychedelic Review*, 1966, 8.

Privette, G. "Peak Experience, Peak Performance, and Flow: A Comparative Analysis of Positive Human Experiences. *Journal of Personality and Social Psychology*, 1983, 45 (6): 1361-68.

Privette, G. and C. M. Bundrick. "Peak Experience, Peak Performance, and Flow: Personal Descriptions and Theoretical Constructs." *Journal of Social Behavior and Personality*, 1991, 6 (5): 169-88.

Quarrick, Gene. *Our Sweetest Hours: Recreation and the Mental State of Absorption*. Jefferson, N. Carolina: McFarland and Co., 1989.

Rahilly, Deborah. "A Phenomenological Analysis of Authentic Experience." *Journal of Humanistic Psychology*, Spring, 1993, 33(2): 49-71.

Rapaport, D. and Gill, M. "The Points of View and Assumptions of Metapsychology." *International Journal of Psychoanalysis*, 1959, 40: 153.

Ravizza, Kenneth. "Peak Experiences in Sport." In the *Journal of Humanistic Psychology,* 1977, 17: 38-9.

Rilke, Rainer Maria. *The Selected Poetry of Rainer Maria Rilke.* New York: Random House, 1982.

Rinpoche, Sogyal. *The Tibetan Book of Living and Dying.* San Francisco: Harper, 1992.

Roberts, Richard. *In the Zone: Self-actualization and the Destabilization of Paradigm Paralysis. An Exploratory Study of the Embodied Total Attention Experience.* CA: Columbia Pacific University: 1997. (Co-researchers: Aaron, Arleen, Brad, Carl, Jeff, John, Liz, Mary, Robin, Tom)

Rogers, Carl. "Actualizing Tendency in Relation to Motives and To Consciousness." In M. R. Jones, Ed., *Nebraska Symposium on Motivation*. Lincoln: University of Nebraska Press, 1963.

Rogers, Carl. *On Becoming a Person: A Therapist's View of Psychotherapy.* Boston: Houghton Mifflin, 1961.

Roshi, Suzuki. *Zen Mind, Beginner's Mind.* New York: Weatherhill, 1970.

Schultz, Duane. *Growth Psychology: Models of the Healthy Personality.* New York: D. Van Nostrand Company, 1977.

Seligman, M. E. P. *Learned Optimism.* New York: Alfred A. Knopf, 1990.

Selye, Hans. *The Stress of Life.* New York: McGraw Hill, 1956.

Shapiro, D. "A Perceptual Understanding of Color Response." In *Rorschach Psychology.* Ed. M. Rickersman. New York: John Wiley and Sons, 1960.

Shapiro, D. & Walsh, R. Eds. *Meditation: Classic and Contemporary Perspectives.* New York: Aldine, 1984.

Sheehan, George. *Running and Being.* New York: Warner, 1978.

Sheehy, Gail. *Passages: Predictable Crises of Adult Life.* New York: E. P. Dutton, 1974.

Sheehy, Gail. *Pathfinders.* New York: Bantam Books, 1981.

Shoham, S. G. *Rebellion, Creativity and Revelation.* New Brunswick: Science Reviews Ltd., 1985.

Solley, C.M. and Murphy, G. *Development of the Perceptual World.* New York: Basic Books, 1960.

Solomons, L. and G. Stein, "Normal Motor Automation." *Psychological Review, 1986,* 36:492-572.

Sperry, R. W. "Consciousness, Personal Identity, and the Divided Brain." *Neuropsychologia,* 1984, 22: 661-73.

Sperry, R. W. "Psychology's Mentalist Paradigm and the Religion/Science Tension." *American Psychologist,* 1988, 43: 607-13.

Spilka, B., Hood, R. and Gorsuch, R. *Psychology of Religion: An Empirical Approach.* Englewood, NJ: Prentice Hall, 1985.

Strube, M., Berry, J. and S. Moergen. "Relinquishment of Control and the Type A Behavior Pattern: The Role of Performance Evaluation." *Journal of Personality and Social Behavior,* 1985, 49: 831-42.

Suzuki, D. *Mysticism: Christian and Buddhist*. New York: Macmillan, 1957.

Tart, Charles. *Altered States of Consciousness*. New York: John Wiley and Sons, 1969.

Tart, Charles. *Waking Up: Overcoming the Obstacles to Human Potential*. Boston: Shambhala Publications, 1986.

Taylor, S. and S. Fiske. "Salience, Attention and Attribution: Top of the Head Phenomena." In Vol. 11 of *Advances in Experimental Social Psychology*, Ed. L. Berkowitz. New York: MacMillan, 1978.

Thomas, L. Eugene and Pamela Cooper. "Incidence and Psychological Correlates of Intense Spiritual Experiences." *Journal of Transpersonal Psychology*, 1980, 12(1).

Thoreau, H. *Walden*. Boston: Houghton, Osgood & Co., 1880.

Titchener, Edward. *Lectures on the Elementary Psychology of Feeling and Attention*. New York: Arno Press, 1973.

Tolstoy, L. "My Confession" (1882), quoted in W. James, *The Varieties of Religious Experience*. New York: New American Library, 1958.

Torrence, E. "A Psychological Study of American Jet Aces." Paper presented at the Western Psychological Association Meeting, Long Beach, California. 1974.

Trungpa, Chogyam. *Cutting Through Spiritual Materialism*. Berkeley: Shambhala, 1973.

Trungpa, Chogyam. *The Myth of Freedom*. Berkeley: Shambhala, 1976.

Tulku, Tarthang. *Skillful Means: Patterns for Success*. Dharma Publishing, 1978.

Underhill, E. *Mysticism: A Study in the Nature and Development of Man's Spiritual Consciousness.* New York: Meridian Press, 1955.

Vaughan, F. *Awakening Intuition.* New York: Doubleday, 1979.

Von Senden, M. *Space and Sight.* Glencoe, Ill.: Free Press, 1960.

Walsh, Roger and Frances Vaughan. "The Art of Transcendence: An Introduction to Common Elements of Transpersonal Practices." *Journal of Transpersonal Psychology*, 1993, 23 (1): 1-10.

Walsh, Roger and Frances Vaughan. Eds. *Paths Beyond Ego: The Transpersonal Vision.* Los Angeles: J. P. Tarcher, 1993.

Wankel, L. "The Importance of Enjoyment to Adherence and Psychological Benefits from Physical Activity. Special Issue: Exercise and Psychological Well-Being." *International Journal of Sport Psychology*, 1993, 24 (2): 151-69.

Watts, Alan. *Meditation.* New York: Pyramid, 1974.

Watts, Alan. *The Book: On the Taboo Against Knowing Who You Are.* New York: Vintage Books, 1972.

Watts, Alan. *The Way of Zen.* New York: Vintage Books, 1957.

Waynbaum, Israel. Trans. from French by Christine Madeleine du Bois, "The Affective Qualities of Perception." In *The Heart's Eye: Emotional Influences in Perception and Attention.* Eds. Niedenthal, Paula M. and Shinobu Kitayama. San Diego: Academic Press, 1994.

Wells, A. "Self-esteem and Optimal Experience." In *Optimal Experience: Psychological Studies of Flow in Consciousness,* Ed. M. Csikszenthihalyi, M. and I. S. Csikszenthihalyi. New York: Cambridge University Press, 1988

Welwood, John. "Befriending Emotion: Self-Knowledge and Transformation." *Journal of Transpersonal Psychology,* 1979, 11: 158.

Werner, H. *Comparative Psychology of Mental Development.* New York: International Universities Press, 1957.

Whalen, S. and M. Csikszentmihalyi. "A Comparison of the Self-Image of Talented Teenagers with a Normal Adolescent Population." *Journal of Youth and Adolescence,* 1989, 18 (2): 131-46.

White, R. W. "Motivation Reconsidered: The Concept of Competence." *Psychological Review,* 1959, 66: 297-333.

Wilber, Ken. *No Boundary: Eastern and Western Approaches to Personal Growth.* Boston: Shambala Publications, 1979.

Wordsworth, William. "Ode on Intimations of Immortality." In *Immortal Poems of the English Language.* Ed. Oscar Williams. New York: Washington Square Press, 1952.

Wuthnow, R. "Peak Experiences: Some Empirical Tests." *Journal of Humanistic Psychology,* 1978, 18 (3): 59-75.

Yogananda, Paramahansa. *Man's Eternal Quest and Other Talks.* Los Angeles: Self-Realization Fellowship, 1975.

Young, Shinzen. *Meditation in the Zone.* Audiotape of lecture by Shinzen Young. Boulder, CO: Sounds True Audio, 1996.

Zukav, Gary. *The Seat of the Soul.* New York: Simon & Schuster, 1989

Additional Resources

Skiboards.com Links

Youtube Page: www.youtube.com/user/Skiboards1

Facebook Page: facebook.com/SkiboardsSuperstore

Twitter: twitter.com/Skiboards

Ebay Store: myworld.ebay.com/skiboardsuperstore/

Amazon Store: www.skiboardssuperstore.com

Video Clips: skiboards.com/index.php?main_page=page&id=12

Skiboards University: skiboards.com/index.php?main_page&id=3

Rentals by Mail: skiboards.com/index.php?main_page=page&id=16

Outlet: SkiboardsOutlet.com

Summit Skiboards: SummitSkiboards.com

Contact Information

U.S & Canada: 800-784-0540
International: +1-970-884-2947
Mailing: 374 Tamara Lane, Unit A, Bayfield, CO 81122
Email: info@skiboards.com

Abstract: Doctoral Dissertation
by Richard (Doc) L. Roberts

In the Zone: Self-Actualization and the Destabilization of Paradigm Paralysis. An Exploratory Study of the Embodied Total Attention Experience.

This study investigated the characteristics, requisite conditions and benefits of the regular and long-term exposure to the zone (an embodied total attention or peak experience). A literature review compared waking consciousness to waking sleep, a sub-optimal state of functioning, associated with the automatization of attention and perception. Paradigm paralysis was postulated to explain this condition, believed to be recognizable by those experiencing the zone, a brief jolt of awakening.

Ten adult amateur athletes (five male and five female, ages 32 to 50), who were involved in various physical activities, served as co-researchers. These individuals experienced the zone on a regular (two to three times a week) and long-term (at least for the past five years) basis. They were interviewed regarding their as-lived experience. Data was classified into fundamental categories according to five research questions and constituents (underlying 'meaning units') derived from the literature. The percentage of responses was calculated.

The zone was determined to be a total attention experience with thirteen of sixteen constituents reported by 80-100% of the co-researchers, being: transience, ineffable, openness, an altered sense of time, fully present, loss of inhibition, intensity, effortlessness, heightened body awareness, insights, peak performance, ego-transcendence and expanded identity (transpersonal self). Csikszentmihalyi's six flow conditions were confirmed by all co-researchers (excepting challenge and skills match with 70%), indicating the zone was repeatable. In addition, 'cessation of thought' (an emergent constituent) was reported by all co-researchers.

The following constituents of paradigm paralysis were reported by 80-100% of co-researchers: mindlessness, limited expression, pessimistic bias, rubricized perception, the persona, waking sleep and related symptoms. The zone, it was concluded, afforded a vantage point for viewing and breaking down (an emergent constituent) limiting mindsets or paradigms leading to temporary 'awakenings' from waking sleep. All co-researchers reported feeling more awake (compared to waking consciousness) and indicated deautomatization, during and after the zone, consistent with the literature.

Results confirmed Maslow's and Csikszentmihalyi's proposals that regular peak experiences led to the development of self-actualizing characteristics with eleven of fourteen constituents being reported by 80% or more: positive affect, self-acceptance, health benefits, openness, Taoist acceptance, desire to increase frequency, ego-transcendence, being present, enhanced performance, loss of inhibition and more creativity. A majority (80% and up) reported experiencing characteristics in Maslow's twelve item checklist.

Summary

The co-researchers in the present study have contributed literally a combined 165 years of personal research regarding their regular experiences of the zone, its characteristics, conditions and benefits. This data adds to a growing number of studies measuring total attention experiences as well as studies specifically of physical activities as a means to precipitate these experiences.

Descriptions of the zone in this study have demonstrated a remarkable similarity to that of the total attention experience found in the literature. It would appear that the zone is a total attention experience, one that is experienced as a result of engaging in particular physical activities. The conditions necessary to entering the zone have been found to parallel those of total attention experiences as outlined by Csikszentmihalyi. The co-researchers in this study particularly noted the cessation of thought as being a primary constituent.

The zone was characterized by a total, one-pointed focus of attention, a fully present moment by moment awareness, such that the usual subject-object dichotomies dissolved. The resulting experience was viewed as leading to ego-transcendence and an experience of an expanded self-identity, termed the Authentic Self.

In addition, experiences of all co-researchers confirmed that the regular experience of the zone contributed certain positive benefits to their lives. Among these benefits was a deautomatization, indicated by a heightened perception that was experienced both during and after the zone. The majority of co-researchers, from the vantage point of the zone, were able to identify specific constituents of paradigm paralysis in their own lives. Co-researchers indicated that they were not only able to gain insights into the limiting mindsets, views or beliefs associated with paradigm paralysis, but that these insights allowed them to make certain changes in their lives to continue to breakdown the inhibitions and limitations associated with paradigm paralysis. This represented an additional emergent constituent in this study.

Implications for Sports Psychology

Research to date points to the conclusion that there is a correlation between the zone, wherein thought processes and ego controls are suspended, and peak performance. Knowledge of the zone could be instrumental in training individuals for superior athletic performance in numerous sports. As the individual becomes absorbed in the experience itself, they're able to transcend ego-involvement and achieve beyond previous limits. The capacity to experience the zone could open up new vistas for amateur and professional athletes.

It is not surprising then that there has been a surge in training techniques derived from Zen mindfulness practices in recent times. Though not presently fully integrated into traditional athletic training programs, these various 'alternative' training methods are gaining in popularity. Adopting the instructions from Zen mindfulness practices to various athletic activities, numerous teachers and sport psychologists have attempted to initiate the experience of the zone, along with its accompanying benefits, on and off the playing field. A proliferation of 'Zen and the Art of' books have provided crossover instruction in sports, such as golf, tennis, skiing, and archery. Instruction involves suggestions such as being here-and-now, paying total attention and 'unlearning' the tendency to be judgmental and self-conscious, thus short-circuiting the normal conscious thought processes, suspending the master codes and breaking old habits. (Gallwey; Herrigel; Nideffer; Sheehan; Young)

What these alternative training approaches emphasize is enjoyment of the experience itself, rather than focusing on the achievement of external rewards. These Zen approaches are essentially methods of training the attention, to circumvent the usual fragmentation and chaotic flow that characterizes waking state. Peak performance is viewed as a byproduct of this mindfulness training. Traditional approaches to training, conversely, often focus on achieving goals, refining skills, and pumping up the motivation, but rarely include how to enjoy the activity and become fully absorbed in the experience.

Yet, it is possible that these traditional training methodologies reinforce ego-involvement and the pursuit of external rewards. They may even generate anxiety and stress over performance as measured by external standards. Some research has suggested that situations that produce stress and anxiety, such as athletic competition, may constrict attention. As a result, important data is overlooked and performance suffers. (Cohen; Easterbrook; Korchin; Lasch) As anxiety increases, as one becomes more involved in ego-based attainments, performance may be negatively effected. Studies have suggested a connection between suspension of thought processes and enhanced performance, and in contrast a link between automatization of thought, perception and behavior and poor performance. (Abelson; Bandura; Langer; Langer & Imber; Pratto; Strube et al.; Taylor & Fiske) These results could be of great benefit to sports psychologists and athletic trainers.

Unfortunately, discussions of the zone are rarely included in athletic training. Current paradigms often dictate that an individual participate in sports to obtain some result, such as developing muscle strength, staying in shape, winning, gaining recognition from others, as a diversion from work. As seen previously, this externalization of attention, directed to egocentric pursuits, disallows the experience of the zone and keeps the individual functioning in the "business of living" consciousness. (Quarrick)

The concept of paradigm paralysis is more often understood in the context of spiritual practices aimed at self-realization, than related to athletic training. Athletic activities have rarely been considered a path to self-realization, yet research may suggest this very possibility. As discussed earlier, athletic activities seem to parallel that of meditation practices, particularly Zen mindful- ness meditation. Athletes, highly skilled at focusing the attention and pushing the limits of potential, possess the ability to "liberate consciousness from the determining force of genetic instructions, of habits, of cultural conditioning." (Csikszentmihalyi)

These ideas represent a promising area of research and explor- ation for sports psychologists, as well as trainers of amateur and professional athletes, and for those individuals who wish to challenge the limits of human performance. Initial studies suggest that athletes who are able to enter the embodied total attention experience not only report peak moments of performance, but numerous beneficial aftereffects, above and beyond what could be expected from exercise alone. This is a relatively new area of research regarding human potentialities.

Conclusion

Aftereffects characteristic of self-actualizing or fully functioning individuals were reported by all co-researchers in this study believed by them to be the result of the regular and long-term experience of the zone.

The zone represents a relatively new area of research. The possibility, that not only meditation and other spiritual disciplines can assist individuals in developing to their true potential, but that these transcendent, embodied total attention experiences may be a vehicle for self-actualization and even self-realization, presents a new twist on existing understanding in the field of humanistic and transpersonal psychology.

This study adds to the decades of research suggesting that growth towards optimal functioning, and even possibly self-realization, can be accelerated by frequent exposure to these peak moments. If indeed, these transcendent moments of total attention represent a distinct state of consciousness, which many investigators have supported, then this is a significant breakthrough in the understanding of human possibility.

Tuning and Maintenance

Tuning

Skiboards are tuned just like skis or snowboards. For maximum glide and to protect your bases from occasional scrapes, wax your bases using either a hot wax (best) or wipe on wax (convenient). You'll also want to make sure your side edges are sharp and free from nicks.

Tune kits are not a necessity, but definitely a convenience. You can always pay more at the local ski resort for what you can do yourself in about 10 minutes. You can then hit the slopes sooner rather than waiting. A proper tune kit usually consists of wax, scraper or brush and buff pad. If it does not have an iron, you will need a cheap iron that you can get from a second hand store.

These kits would allow you to hot wax your own bases and save money from having a ski tech at the resort do it. Three temperature wax packages are best so you can choose which to use depending on the existing conditions. Hot waxing is easy to do.

There are also wipe-on waxes that allow you to just wipe it on, let it dry and buff. You can use a hair dryer to melt the wax after you wipe it on for a better wax job. Then let it dry and buff (even a paper towel will do).

Another handy tool is the edge tuner. These allow you to sharpen your edges. This is good periodically, but especially when icy conditions exist. Edge tuners usually fit easily in a backpack, carry bag or even your pocket.

If you want true consistent performance and long lasting durability, I suggest keeping your skiboards in prime shape. Here are some basic tips:

At the very least, you want to wipe off the water or snow from your skiboards before placing them in a bag or trunk. Especially make sure the steel edges are dry. The slightest moisture can create a little rust.

Carry bags are recommended to make sure your skiboards are not dinged during transport. These are great for protecting your skiboards (put them in with bases facing each other).

In addition, it helps to ride your skiboards a shoulder width apart. This stance keeps them from banging together as that creates nicks and chips. Also, try not to bang them together while sitting on the lift.

Tuning Tips:

Edges

Make sure your edges are smooth and sharp. Here are a few tips for keeping your edges in good condition. First, inspect your edges when you inspect your skiboard bases.

Sharper, smoother edges means better grip when carving. Your edges can get dulled by snow abrasiveness, ice, dirt, hard objects (rocks, metal stakes, etc.) or by accidentally slapping or scissoring tips together in a turn.

Of course, if your edge damage is major (bent or broken), it's time to seek out a good repair shop or get a new pair.

It's easiest and least expensive (compared to going to a ski shop) to buy a pocket edger. These fit easily into, well, a pocket and can be used to run along the edges to smooth them out. Usually there is an option for 90 or 88 degrees depending on your side bevel. You just want to run it in one direction tip to tail. It doesn't take very long – one minute or two.

Detuning

If you have brand new skiboards, you may want to consider detuning your tip and tail edges. With new skiboards, the edges are sharp all along both sides. Sharp edges, not detuned, can create a wobbling feeling at first, as the edges are grabby when new. This is especially true when they have aggressive side bevels, such as 89 or 88 degrees.

Now sometimes, to be able to break out of one turn and move into the next, it's easier if the edges are dulled a bit in certain places. Detuning means rounding out the edges about 1 inch before and up to 1 inch after they leave the ground. Measure this distance putting them flat on the floor. Use a regular file or the file from your edge tuner. Use a one directional motion and just be easy on the pressure.

With detuning, the idea is to dull the sharpness, not take the edge off completely. Do the same on both tip sides as well as the same area along the back tips. Detuning makes for easier spinning, turning and going backwards. Your skiboards will still hold an edge at speed and give stability in lay over carves. With just a little time invested, it will make a huge difference in turning from edge to edge faster. Of course, normal riding will eventually wear these areas, so it's up to you.

Waxing

Base materials, either extruded or sintered, are made of low friction material so water will not stick as easily. However, the bases of your skiboards will glide best when water beads (meaning small droplets of water) form under the base acting like small ball bearings. This enables the skiboard to glide faster. Wax serves this purpose.

Wax also helps to protect the base from oxidation. When oxidized, the base won't bead water and becomes slow and sticky. Ultra Violet rays radiating off the snow contribute to the oxidation process and a subsequent breakdown in the polyethylene base.

Wax helps skiboards to go faster, ride smoother and it protects your bases.

There are two good methods to wax your bases.

1) Wipe On Waxes

This is definitely the fastest method. You can usually just use an applicator with a good wipe on wax. Let it dry and go ride. That's the idea.

However, even better is warming your bases, in your room or near a heater. Wipe on the wax, let it dry and buff (even with a paper towel) to smooth it out.

The best method though is to use a hair dryer with wipe on wax. First warm your bases with the hair dryer, then wipe on the wax from tip to tail. Now melt the wax into the bases with your hair dryer. Let it dry. Then, buff. This method is almost like a hot wax, but easier and more convenient, especially when traveling.

Not all wipe on waxes are the same. What you want is one with a high wax content. High Velocity Wax (available on skiboards.com) fits the bill.

Lastly, and the easiest by far, are the teflon applications such as Zardoz Notwax. This can be applied while you are on the lift and can be used over wax for maximum speed. It is intended mostly for normal or warmer conditions and not for extreme cold. Depending on conditions, Zardoz may need to be applied up to two or three times a day. It is not intended to protect your bases, but simply to improve glide.

2) Hot Waxes

Hot waxing is absolutely the best method for improving glide and protecting your bases. Hot waxes penetrate the base and make for the smoothest ride. It takes a little more time than wipe on waxing. For this you will want hot wax, an iron, a scraper or brush and buff pad. As it can be somewhat messy, you will want to have at least papers under your skiboards.

The goal here is to fill the pores of your board with wax giving you a smooth ride, better performance, and of course, SPEED. Extruded bases, a little less porous are less expensive bases, and do not hold as much wax. If you have extruded bases, you will just want to wax more often.

The other type of base is sintered. It is a more porous material and holds wax better, equating to greater speed. Either way, use your correct temperature wax (usually there is a range indicated on the wax). Our special formula Glide-On wax is for artic, cold and medium temperature conditions with specific temperature ranges for each.

1. Place your boards on a stable surface. Turn on and adjust your iron – medium to low heat.

2. Hold the iron so the hot surface is up with the point towards you. Hover the iron tip two inches over the board and apply the wax to the hot surface of the iron. The wax will drip on the bases of your skiboards. Keep it moving.

3. Move the iron lengthwise smoothly dripping a line down the rail 1/4" inside the edge, around the tip, back up the other rail, around the tail, and back up the center of the board. You don't need to use too much, but of course not too little. This is the trickiest part of hot waxing.

4. When done dripping wax on the base, now rest the flat of the iron on the bases and move it from tip to tail melting the wax into a thin layer. KEEP THE IRON MOVING. Make sure the wax melts and smoothes out and covers the entire base area. Remember if you leave a hot iron on a spot on your base for more than a few seconds, you are looking at an expensive hole.

5. You may need to run it tip to tail again to make sure all the wax drippings are smoothed out. It should not take more than a couple minutes to smooth it out.

6. Allow 30 minutes or more to dry thoroughly. Of course, do both boards.

7. After dry, use a scraper (usually has an indented edge for this) to remove wax from you edges. If no indented edge, then use the scraper as is to remove wax from your edges.

8. Once the wax is off your edges, then use the scraper to remove the excess wax from your bases. This is messy, so have something underneath. Usually it's easier to hold the skiboard upright and run the scraper down the base. You don't want to press too hard, but you do want to create a smooth, flat wax coating. You are basically removing all bumps or pockets of excess wax. This may take a few minutes per board.

9. If you don't have a scraper, then use a wire brush (often one or the other is included in a tune kit). Brush until smooth.

10. Finally, using a buff pad, you want to buff the bases until you get a real slick, smooth base. This polishes the wax job.

11. Most new skis do not come waxed. They may have a factory wax which is a thin layer of wipe on wax. This wears off quickly.

Stripping? Some say stripping the old wax off with a base cleaner is best to remove the dirt and debris. Others would say that you just wax over the other layer. While you may not want to strip each time you hot wax, periodically, you may want to do this. It is at your discretion. There are many wax strippers on the market.

How often to wax? Depends on how often you go. It is best to just inspect your bases. If the wax is wearing off, you will see it. Time to wax again.

If you're feeling lazy, take your skiboards to a local ski shop and pay them to do it. What you want though is a hot wax by hand. Sometimes shops use a wax machine that does a great job, but is not as good as a hand wax and does not last as long.

Base Work

If you get tears in the bases or pits, you may need some base work. Sometimes you can smooth out some tears with a razor blade and then cover with a good hot wax. Other times, if the bases need more professional care, you can either take them to a local ski shop or try p-tex on your bases. Do not ride your skiboards if the inner core is exposed.

To p-tex yourself, assuming you have p-tex sticks, light one end and rotate to drip into the hole. Gravity will pull the p-tex down. Over fill the hole slightly.

Allow the p-tex to dry for approximately 20 minutes. Use a razor or Metal Scraper to make the weld flush. Slice tip to tail. A quality effort will increase speed. You will definitely want to do a hot wax after you're done.

Boot Care

Make sure that you dry the inner liners of your ski boots after skiboarding. This prevents molds and fungus from growing. Pull out the liners and let them dry at room temperature. Also, store the boots with buckles latched so they will hold their shape. One more tip is to keep your boots warm when heading to the mountains, as they will fit better and go on easier at the resort.

One handy device is a set of boot warmers, like Happy Feet Dry'n'Warm. If you're riding more than one day in a row, you may want your boots to be dry by the next morning. Just a thought! Sometimes depending on your situation, you can't just pull out the liners and have them dry by the next morning. These boot dryers are very effective and inexpensive.

Excerpts from The Press

Following are a few excerpts from the press regarding the sport of skiboarding. For the full articles and press releases related to skiboarding, visit the Skiboards.com University section.

"Mini Skis – The Next Type of Snowriding?" In *Hyperski Magazine*

These [skiboards] could put a major dent in the income of ski instructors. These are the easiest form of downhill snow travel to master. These enhance freedom for every skier willing to try something new. These are skiboards. These are between 40 cm and 90 cm and clamp onto your regular ski boot in either releasable or non-release bindings. No need for poles; no worries about crossing skis; no need for a week of lessons. Yes, you can use poles with miniskis, but there is no need to since unweighting comes easily.

"Park Rangers" In *Skiing Magazine*

"I started down the hill, waiting for the inevitable slam. But it didn't come. I began to carve and bank and slice. Something about this felt familiar. Then it dawned on me: I wasn't skiing, I was skating. These little skis had jogged some hidden muscle memories. We all began experimenting with how far over we could lean in a carve. I was astonished at how well the edges held. Soon I was laying out horizontally, as if carving heel-side on a snowboard. These are a kick in the ass! This changes the whole paradigm. This is the beginning of the future of skiing. These are fun after five minutes. We can't stop now, this is the most fun I've ever had on skis."

"'Bumps for Boomers' groomed for balance" In *Denver Post*

SNOWMASS - If you're a baby boomer who avoids moguls and powder at all costs, but you're increasingly intimidated by how fast others are tearing past you on the groomed runs, Joe Nevin has a way out of your dilemma.

Leave your conventional skis in the garage and let him give you a "Bumps for Boomers" lesson using ski boards, those funny-looking mini-skis that are just over 3 feet long.

One student told Nevin she liked ski boards because learning on them was no longer a matter of the brain telling the feet what to do.

"When she put the ski boards on, the information flow was completely reversed," Nevin said. "She was feeling things in her feet, the information was coming up to her brain and she was processing it."

Nevin sees ski boards as learning tools, but some students like them so much they never go back to their conventional skis. They're fun, and they're easier on boomer knees.

Liz Flanagan, a former "terminal intermediate" from Snowmass Village, said ski boards have opened up the entire mountain to her - from double black diamond mogul runs to halfpipes.

"I have so much fun on these, I prefer to ski on these," said Flanagan, 60. "I ski with friends who are not on them, and I don't have any trouble keeping up with them. As long as you're in balance, you can do it."

———————

"Skiboards.com Superstore Makes Splash from Bayfield" In *Farmington Herald*

Richard "Doc" Roberts knew it was time to expand his business after a customer in Sweden called him at 3 a.m. to order a skiboard from his company, Skiboards Superstore, then located just outside Boulder in his garage.

Since that call in the late 1990s, Roberts has expanded in Bayfield, now home to one of the world's largest skiboard retailers on the Internet, through skiboards.com.

Neither a ski nor a snowboard, a skiboard has nearly the same surface area as a ski, but with prices in the $250 range (including bindings) – about half the cost. Roberts said skiboards can go anywhere skis go, but without the steep learning curve.

Roberts said the problem selling skiboards historically is that major ski brands such as K2 put their name on skiboards, but for the most part the industry doesn't know what to do with the item. It's the same phenomenon that happened when snowboards came on the scene, he said.

"There has been very little promotion in the ski industry for skiboards," Roberts said.

Although "Doc" has a doctorate in sports psychology and is an avid skier, he learned how to run a business in the field. "The Internet was the only way to offer the selection of skiboards," he said. It was also necessary for a startup company with no advertising or marketing budget.

"It was the only way to reach the markets nationally and internationally," Taylor said. Many customers are on the East Coast, but orders are regularly shipped to Canada, United Kingdom, Korea, Japan, Australia, Chili and New Zealand.

————————

"Skiboards.com – Online Store for Ski Industry's Latest Trend" In *Four Corners Business Journal*

Bayfield, CO – Skiboards. They're all over the slopes, strapped to the feet of an increasing number of folks who relish the thrill of shushing down a mountain. On the flip side, they are noticeably absent in ski or snowboard retail shops across the nation.

So what's an enthusiast – or an intrigued novice – to do? Quite simply, go online to skiboards.com, the Bayfield based resource for retail purchase and information about these increasingly popular mini-boards – an inventive hybrid of skates and traditional downhill and cross-country skis. With a ski industry slow to embrace and promote a new sporting discipline and its equipment, the Internet has proven incredibly effective, with thousands of devotees pointing and clicking their way to skiboard heaven.

Most orders come in over the Internet, though Roberts acknowledges that customers will call to make certain they purchase the proper boards. Fat, thin, shaped, loner, short, the options abound, and Roberts and crew will tailor the customer's purchase to the type of terrain, be it hard-pack, powder or anything in between. Backcountry skiboards are also growing in popularity.

"We have people putting 3-year olds on these," said Roberts, holding a miniature Salomon skiboard recommended for children up to about 4 ft. 10 in. tall. "I put my son on these and within one day he was already in a double black (expert runs) in the trees. He'd never been on a ski lift, on snow or anything. You don't really need to learn how to snowplow because you don't have the big tips. These turn quickly and they stop quickly. A lot of moms who have told us that they usually end up sitting in the lodge while their family is up on the slopes can now go anywhere that their family does! These moms are finally having fun on the slopes!"

———————

"It's a board! It's a ski!" In *Rocky Mountain News*

A new snow sport is sliding its way into the hearts of skiers, snowboarders and even inline skaters. It's called skiboarding or snowblading and it combines the best aspects of all three activities. Snowblades or skiboards are shorter, wider and more curved than traditional skis, allowing users to turn as they would on skis, ski backwards as they can on inline skates and perform the same acrobatic stunts that snowboarders do. They can be used with or without poles and work with snowboard, ski or mountaineering boots. They're so fun, and they really allow people to use the whole mountain," said Dan O'Connell, director of the children's center at Winter Park and a professional skiboard racer.

O'Connell said skiboarding is also extremely easy to learn. A skier or snowboarder can typically catch on after day and can advance to other levels quickly. Several ski resorts, including Winter Park, are also using the snowblades to help teach skiing. "It reinforces certain movements and it lets them go out the snow and have fun in a non-intimidating way."

"Wide and short skis promise easy fun" In *Denver Post*

BAYFIELD - If you haven't already seen them, you will soon.

Skiboards are growing in popularity the way snowboards did a couple of decades ago.

Best described as skis that are half as long and twice as wide, skiboards allow just about anybody with an interest in gravity-based snow sports to enjoy them, said Doc Roberts, owner of Skiboards Superstore in Bayfield.

Ease of learning is one of the highlights of skiboards, and they're easier on the body, Roberts said.

"Skiboards are just so gosh darn easy anybody can do them and enjoy themselves," Komie said. "You don't need poles. They're totally fun."

"The majority of our market is families," Roberts said. "Moms and dads can go with their kids and pretty much go anywhere." Roberts said some people switch to skiboards because of age or bad knees. Cost is another reason.

"Short and Sweet" In *The Professional Skier*

No, it's not really a joke. It's a pretty accurate account of what happened at last year's Team Training at Copper Mountain, Colorado. America's elite instructors left their skis in the rack, stashed their poles, and went out on skiboards: twin-tip skis (i.e., shovels at both ends) of 100 centimeters or less with non-release bindings.

It was supposed to be little more than a get-acquainted session with a new product that seemed set to make a 'Splash. But the D-Teamers decided the skiboards were too much fun, and they just didn't want to take them off.

"Everyone was laughing so hard, but they were learning too," reports team "member Mermer Blakeslee. "Skiboards demand an open form of teaching. You can't stand around and talk. All the Demo Team people are real doers - everyone just took off and had a great time learning. When they needed help they asked for it."

Even Britain's Prince Charles and his sons William and Harry have taken a liking to skiboarding, having been introduced to the sport last season at the Whistler-Blackcomb Resort in, Canada, So enamored were they of skiboards that they ended up taking a pair back to Buckingham Palace with them.

The appeal of the skiboard is simple. With its remarkable maneuverability, the skiboard shines in moguls, glades, and even terrain parks, making it the perfect tool for today's ski resort-*cum*-winter playground.

But first, a history lesson. Like longboard skiing, the skiboard traces its roots back to Europe, where it was borne of necessity as basic transportation. Alpine mountain guides, needing to traverse snowfields and avalanche chutes in the late spring and summer, would hacksaw a pair of skis down to 70 centimeters or so, attach a pair of strap-on bindings that would work with hiking or mountaineering boots, and stuff these homemade snow toys, called "figls" in their packs.

"It's an alternative gliding activity," counters Al Marino, product manager at Salomon. "It's not skiing, it's not snowboarding, it's something else."

As a teaching aid, skiboards; could have their most significant impact on accomplished skiers. "The potential for the tool is phenomenal," says Irwin. With their deep sidecuts, skiboards allow skiers to experience a true carved turn at low speeds. With their short turning radius, they make upper-lower body separation a breeze and can help even the most bump-phobic skier tackle the moguls with confidence.

Skiboards are likely to prove especially popular at mid-size mountains, where their turn-happy nature makes small runs ski bigger and busy trails often make high speeds impractical. "When it's crowded on the slope, you can turn it quicker," says Jochl. "You don't have to go as fast to have fun. You can do a helicopter or other tricks without worrying about getting hurt."

About Richard L. Roberts, PhD.

Richard L. Roberts, Ph.D., is a Human Potential Consultant and national seminar leader. He has presented his empowering seminars throughout the U.S. since 1979 in the field of vocational awakening, internet marketing, instant skiing, peak performance and self-actualization.

Education:

Dr. Roberts has a Bachelors Degree in Physiological Psychology from the State University of New York at Stony Brook. He has a Master of Science Degree in Vocational Counseling/Assessment from the State University of New York at Oswego and a Doctoral Degree from Columbia Pacific University in Psychology, emphasis Human Potential.

Experience:

Dr. Roberts has personally assisted 10's of thousands of individuals to discover and fulfill their full potential. He offers a rare combination of practical real-world knowledge in personal transformation and prosperity generating strategies, with an in-depth, intuitive understanding of what it takes for individuals to discover their talents, engage their true destinies and self-actualize.

In his extensive career, Dr. Roberts has served as a corporate consultant and workshop leader, creating many custom tailored personal enrichment programs. Among the companies he has presented to are the following:

- Ventura County Government
- Ericsson Communications
- CalComp
- Northrop
- Off Duty Enterprises
- A.T.& T.
- Security Pacific
- Allstate Insurance
- Small Business Administration
- N. Orange County Community
- U. S. Department of Education
- Indian Hills Community College
- University of Colorado – Boulder
- Colorado Department of Revenue
- Chicago Title
- Hughes Aircraft
- Vector Electronics
- Sunstrand Aviation
- BASF
- Warner-Lambert
- Colonial Insurance
- Security Pacific
- Donnelly Marketing
- U.S. Postal Service
- Chicago Title
- Chapman University
- Boulder Valley Schools
- Fort Lewis College

Dr. Roberts also created the Breakthrough Club, a community of individuals committed to self-actualizing and realizing their career potential. The Breakthrough Club principles and guidelines are now incorporated into the *Discover Your Life's Work Seminar and Guidebook* as well as *Instant Skiing, Instant Fun.*

Additional Experience:

Dr. Roberts is president of the Skiboards Superstore, Inc. (Skiboards.com) an online retail business that represents a unique snow riding sport. The Skiboards Superstore, Inc. is a business that grew out of Dr. Robert's own personal work with the Discover Your Life's Work system that resulted in the creation of a unique niche Internet business. He now teaches and incorporates many of the same principles in his ongoing seminars and publications.

He is also president of Summit Skiboards, a skiboards manufacturing company with worldwide distribution. Summit manufacturing provides a steady source of quality product with active control over all construction details, thus delivering maximum skiboard performance.

In addition, he is manager of Windrider Institute, LLC, a publishing company. The company's mission is to guide as many individuals as possible to awaken to their Higher Calling and to realize their true potential. Windrider Institute Press publishes books focused to enabling individuals to become self-actualizing.

Publications by Richard L. Roberts, Ph.D.

INSTANT SKIING – INSTANT FUN Skiboards: Best Kept Secret on the Slopes

This book provides the inside scoop on the new sport of skiboarding, including not only specific tips on learning to ski instantly with skiboards, but also the relatively unknown transformational shifts that occur when riding the slopes.
(Available at: skiboards.com)

DISCOVER YOUR LIFE'S WORK The Step-by-step Guide To Awaken Your True Vocation & Extraordinary Potential - Create Unbounded Prosperity Fulfilling Your Divine Destiny

This is a self-guided process for discovering your true talents and work that you're best suited for. This is the path to greater prosperity and making a difference with your life. This book is the culmination of over 30 years of individual and group work with thousands of individuals.
(Available at: DiscoverYourLifesWork.com &
VocationalAwakening.com)

DISCOVER YOUR INTERNET NICHE & CREATE YOUR OWN AUTOMATIC CASH MACHINE: Cash In Getting Your Passion Online

This book is an outreach of Dr. Roberts' mission to identify and express your passion on the Internet, create greater prosperity, while also making your unique contribution. Numerous resources are offered for identifying niche markets, driving web traffic and maximizing internet marketing.
(Available at: VocationalAwakening.com & Skiboards.com)

ePUBLISHING NONFICTION FOR MAXIMUM PROFIT

This book guides you through understanding the new ebook publishing market and how to make money selling information on the internet. The focus is on preparing, publishing and marketing your ebook.
(Coming soon at: VocationalAwakening.com & Skiboards.com)